FRENCH
LICENSE

Joe Start

A travel memoir

First published by Start Going Places, 2017

Copyright © 2018 Joe Start

Credits: Front Cover- Madison Shirazi | Photos: Philippe Comelera, Joe Start

Illustrations: © OpenStreetMap contributors; AccidentSketch diagrams, John Reid

ISBN-13: 978-0-9993542-0-9

To the Creative Badger, the Original Handyman and
the Dancing Princess

Table of Contents

Post-scriptum

CHAPTER ONE

Borne 00 - Immigration and Transportation

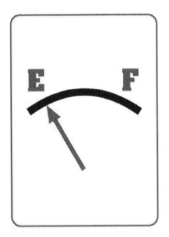

Immigration et Transportation

Oh, to be from Iowa...
Or South Carolina. Or Arkansas. Or Maryland.
Colorado or New Hampshire or Wisconsin would also do.

Or Botswana for that matter. Togo. Swaziland for cryin' out loud. If I came from any of these places, this book wouldn't exist.

But I'm not. I'm from California. I know that doesn't elicit much sympathy, nor should it for many aspects. Sunshine, startups, and such. Wine, cheese and an appreciation for the culinary arts, like Wahoo's fish tacos! An open, cosmopolitan, left-leaning society.

France, where I now reside, has most of these things, too. Both are great places to live, and popular destinations for tourists. 85 million people travelled to France in 2015, making it the world's top draw. 3.6 million of them were Americans. 17 million foreigners visited California that same year, and 441,000 of them were French.

In fact, while each is quite diverse, both California and France share a multitude of similitude. In surface area, topography, and climate they are alike. Both have tall mountains and craggy coasts. Each shoreline extends for a comparable stretch of miles. Both experience heavy snowfall, vicious winds, hail, and sweltering heat waves. Both have crowded freeways zooming between big cities, and meandering dirt paths in the desolate countryside.

Both California and France are leaders in deploying personal transport innovation. Tesla's all-electric auto plant is in Fremont, California. California is the top US market, and France is the top European market for electric vehicle sales. The French have bought 100 000 electric cars already. So, it's no wonder that Tesla recently opened showrooms in France, and that France's €60 000 Autolib' electric cars are coming to municipalities in Cali. Renamed 'Blue California,' drivers in the Golden State will be the first in

America to pick up an electric car for short errands from convenient street spots as easily as taking a shopping cart.

A massive infrastructure build of 100 000 plug-in points should be completed by 2020, ensuring there isn't a zone in the whole of France farther than 40 kilometers from an electric car charging station. Compare that with 16 000 charging stations in the US today. The world's first 'solar panel road' opened 2017 in France at Tourouvre-au-Perche in Normandy. Another road, in Versailles Satory, promises to charge your electric car as you drive, without contact. The Paris region just voted in an 'intelligent route' fund of €60 million to build the kinds of carpool lanes you see in California, plus quieter roads and modular speed control to avoid bottlenecks.

California, home to the headquarters of Google and Uber, is a testing ground for self-driving vehicles. Some would say battleground, after Uber released such cars on the streets of San Francisco before the local authorities granted approval. In Paris, an automated minibus started in January 2017 running on the bridge between the Austerlitz and Lyon train stations. A similar vehicle launched in Issy-les-Moulineaux and still another electric people-mover runs on the parvis of La Défense. In 2018, you'll be able to visit the garden of Versailles in one of a fleet of self-driving cars.

However, one crucial thing the two governments do **NOT** have in common is reciprocal recognition of their drivers' aptitude. In my home state, French drivers, or any *foreign license holder* over 18, for that matter, "may drive in California without getting a California Driver's License as long as their home state driver's license is valid."

However, on French roads, Californian drivers are considered a menace to society. They're tolerated as vacationers renting a Mégane for a month to meander through the Loire Valley. But if they stick around for a year, they must bend to the administration. They must go through the process of obtaining a new legal document, a French license to drive.

What they don't tell you is that it's impossible to complete the whole process from scratch in 12 months.

For some foreign permit holders, there's a quicker route to a French Driver's License. If your country has an accord with France, you simply hand over your current State's license, and they give you a French one. No questions asked. No written test. No driving test. Piece of cake. For me it was, "Let him eat cake!"

This easy peasey exchangey happens with more than *100 countries*, some of which you'd expect, like the 27 other EU nations. This simple license switcheroo takes place if you're from Ireland, where the road rises to meet you... on the left-hand side. Or the Netherlands... where there isn't a paved road higher than *322 meters* above sea level. Or Malta, which hasn't seen a snowflake since… ever!

Nations you wouldn't expect to be on the automatic exchange list include a motley crew of Ethiopia, Morocco, Saudi Arabia, Mozambique, Togo, Botswana, Sierra Leone and Madagascar.

Ethiopia?! Seriously? The capital, Addis Abeba has less than 30 traffic lights. Instead they have 500 traffic police. With that ratio, drivers don't need to watch where they're going, they can wait for someone to point it out to them. Ethiopian drivers routinely steer right into another car or pedestrian. In 2013, 5% of **all** cars in the country were involved in a **FATAL** accident. Watch any 20 cars going by and one's got blood on their bumper.

Fatalities are no big thing to Moroccan drivers. In Morocco, you can run over one person with your car, and continue driving. You can kill a second person, and *still* keep on driving. Only after the *third* fatality will they take away your license.

Really, Saudi Arabia, where women couldn't drive until 2017? Are the male Saudi drivers really prepared to share French roads with women? Saudi Arabia is also dry and dusty with dunes and craters. In other words, if you come from a place that looks like the surface of the moon, you've earned the precious *sésame*.

If Bob Dylan would like to spend some time in Mozambique, it had better be in an armored tank. Their road fatality rate per inhabitant is *six times* that of France's. So is Togo's, which unlike their namesake San Jose sandwich place, serves their pastrami special as pedestrians on pavement. It's five times more deadly than France in Botswana, Sierra Leone and Madagascar, where apparently they hand out licenses to zoo animals with celebrity voices.

For the *US and Canada*, the license transfer is even more arbitrary. Only *certain states* and provinces are allowed the exchange. Arkansas, yes. Kansas, no. Oklahoma, where the wind comes whistling down the plains, which are navigated on straight, flat streets and strictly right-angle turns, is one of these places. Driving on a simple grid with clear sightlines still doesn't prevent Okie drivers from a fatal crash rate twice that of California.

Another exchange state is Delaware, which has no mountains like the Alps. Delaware has no mountains nor molehills to speak of, as the state is 60 feet above sea level.

Delaware has no roundabouts. But if you have a yellow Delaware driver's license, you can trade it even-up for a pink French one.

Florida is also flat as a pancake, and doesn't ever get snow. Nevertheless, your Sunshine State card is a free ticket to clamber your camping car up the *Alpe d'Huez* in a blizzard.

I'm not one of those lucky Floridians. I'm a Californian who moved to France.

This should give me an advantage, because the California road experience resembles most of the driving conditions you find in France. California has roads along cliffs in Big Sur, the *crookedest street*- Lombard in San Francisco, bridges high (like Foresthill) and long (the San Mateo bridge). California has the *Donner Pass*.

You may be surprised to discover California also has 20 *roundabouts* and 50 more to come. France remains the world champion, with 30 000 roundabouts. It is a French invention, after all. *Co-co-ri-co*.

So, California roads are very comparable to the French terrain. France boasts the world's highest viaduct the *Viaduc de Millau*- a 2 1/2 kilometer structure 343 meters above emptiness blown by vicious winds, Europe's highest road- the *Col de la Bonnette* at 2807 meters, the *lacets de Montvernier*- 18 switchbacks in the Savoie Alps, the *passage du Gois* which is covered by the sea and can only be crossed for three hours twice daily at low tide, and France's steep *Col de Turini*.

But as a bonus, California streets pose many unique challenges unknown to France. In San Francisco, you've got to know how to start from an e-break stop pointing up a *30% grade hilltop* when the light turns green in bumper-to-bumper without rolling backwards. Oh, and curbing your wheels when parallel parking on an incline. California has *5-stack overpasses* and *26-lane highway interchanges*, the highest and the widest on the globe. California drivers know how to turn right on a red light safely. Los Angeles is the world's largest car market with 6.5 million vehicles. California municipalities boast more cars per capita than any region on the planet.

California prepares their drivers to take on practically any meteorological condition, whether fog or hail or snow. A California driver would be at home behind the wheel in a *French storm*. A bit of *brouillard de Chantilly* ain't got nuthin' on the fog that accumulates routinely in the Sunset district of San Francisco during a Summer day on the Bay. Not to mention every Thanksgiving the wall of fog you hit winding down in-between the hills of the *Grapevine* on the way to pea soup *Andersen's*.

These challenges make California drivers more prepared to take on tricky road situations elsewhere in the world. This readiness prevents traffic fatalities, making California one of the safest places to drive in the USA- safer than 14 of the US states with French license reciprocal agreements.

What's more, because there are much fewer public transportation alternatives, the average Cali dude has many more kilometers on his keester: nearly double the annual miles driven by a French driver.

None of this mattered to the French administration. For want of a loophole, this California driver had to go back, Jack, do it again, wheels turnin' round and round. Loopholes are great when you're the one who slips through.

Me, I got the noose.

CHAPTER TWO

Borne 25 - Heat wave

Canicule

I didn't know the fun that awaited me when I first arrived in Paris during the summer of '03. Folks here remember that as the '*canicule*' or heat wave. More than 19 000 people died from heat stroke, mostly older people. They didn't make much noise as they melted into the floors of their apartments without air conditioning. So, my family and I weren't aware of the horror going on behind closed doors around us. All we knew is that it was very quiet. And extremely hot.

We were told to expect that in the Summer many Parisians would be on vacation, but this was ridiculous. Le

Vésinet, our suburb in the Yvelines was a ghost town, a museum of empty buildings, and we were the only visitors. We'd walk past cars with advertisements all over them. Their owners received €400 per month toward their car payments by plastering their entire vehicle with stickers for Gauloise cigarettes, or Bouygues mobile phone service or Pelforth beer, so long as they circulated so consumers could get a good look at them. In that long, hot Summer, I saw these cars parked in the same place for weeks.

Even in the busiest of times, Le Vésinet is still sleepy. It was a refuge from the big city for wealthy 19th-century Parisians. As soon as the train tracks were laid out here in 1837, grandiose mansions were built on expansive plots with high stone fences and wrought-iron gates.

We strolled the wide sidewalks and yellow dried lawns without crossing a soul. Our then 3-year-old boy, Paul, was so happy one day to see a cat, probably abandoned, that he ran up to pet it. It scratched him, and he was shocked and saddened. Not from the pain, but from loneliness.

There wasn't another kid to play with in the whole town. So my wife, Aurore, quickly sped him out to a friend's place in the countryside to be with other children. She was already sick of moving furniture and painting. I was left to finish setting up the residence to make it habitable.

The abode that I had found for us was a tiny 500 ft.² '*maison de gardien*' they call them. It's a sort of mini-house built for the caretakers, detached from the main residence, which was a comfortable three-story family home. The lot with the two homes was formerly attached to an even larger mansion on a bigger plot next-door. Sometime ago the person who inherited the huge mansion sold off a section of his lot, the part with the house his groundskeeper lived in. The new plot was so big there was still room to build another huge house in front. This became 14 *bis*.

Bis means 'also.' That's because there was already a number 14 for that street- the 19th century mansion. The original city planners assigned lots next to each other a two digit difference in address no matter how big the lots were. This left no room for new numbers when the lots were split up. This is very common in suburban areas in the countryside in France. Yet another subdivision was called 14 '*ter*,' which is kind of like third. This makes it very fun on a hot day in the middle of August, when you arrive relieved at the number you were seeking, only to learn the house is still two doors down.

I don't know what our landlord Pascal was thinking when he saw me at his gate for the first time. French property owners are particularly suspicious, and the burden is on the renter to prove their viability. This is because it's practically impossible to evict someone. From November to April, known as the '*trève hivernale*' it's literally forbidden to kick them out, even if they don't pay rent.

I had no employment contract at the time, nor did my wife. And we were asking for a one-year lease, considered unreliably short by local standards. Three years was the norm, and practically unbreakable. Both renter and landlord were taking a leap of faith. Probably what sealed it was that Pascal was interested in other cultures, and an American was exotic enough to have as a neighbor. That, and the fact that my wife's parents co-signed, accepting full responsibility if we bailed. Imagine that in the 'States, an able-bodied couple in their 30s having to get retired folks to guarantee their contract?

Our maison de gardien had a regular door but all the windows had thin glass panes, and no curtains. This made it like an oven inside during the canicule when outside it was already over 100°F. I had to put up four sets of curtains fast and install two ceiling fans. There was no way that this could be done during the day. It was too hot.

One of the great things about summer in Europe is the days are so long. The latitude of Paris is about the same as that of Montréal. It's the Gulf Stream winds which make the temperature milder. The other side of the coin is that the sun comes up at 5:30 a.m. For an hour before that, the *twilight* is enough to read by. Without curtains, I was getting a maximum of five hours' sleep a night. Exhaustion was creeping up on me and I wasn't thinking straight.

To begin home improvements, I had to wait until 10:00 p.m. when the sun was down fully, but there was still an hour of twilight. With a flashlight in my mouth and slippery screws on my sweaty fingers, I found some way to put the curtains and fans up without any power tools. It wasn't the most level job ever, but they stayed up, and I finally had some relief. Amazing what you can do when you have to.

The interior was now breezy and cooler, but we still didn't have telephone, TV or internet. I had to take the regional train network, the RER, three stops and pay €3 an hour to check my e-mail at an internet café. Later, I discovered free Wi-Fi at a place a bit farther out: McDonald's. I hadn't eaten at a McDo for years, and here I was visiting daily, sitting at a very uncomfortable seat, listening to that "All we ever want is more, money" song you couldn't seem to get away from in August 2003.

My wife and son returned to a somewhat more

livable accommodation. But we still didn't have our personal belongings. Our 30 boxes shipped from California had been sitting on a pallet in storage somewhere in Paris for a week and a half, while we assembled all they paperwork customs needed, (and the extra 400 euros) that we weren't told about when sending from the US.

In order for me to work in France, I needed to prove my wife is French. In France you have two forms of ID: a passport, and a '*carte d'identité,*' or ID card. A driver's license doesn't count for identification. The first of Aurore's was current, but guess which one they needed? Yep, the second one. No problem, just re-up the old one and we're in business, right? Wrong, it took a MONTH for her to get the new ID card.

One day, every single thing we tried to do didn't work, from paperwork, to finding mechanics closed, to frying my printer brought over from America. I didn't have the grounding prong in the voltage converter. We decided to eat out and give ourselves a couple gifts: a combo TV/ DVD/VCR player and a European voltage printer/ scanner/copier. Handing over our American Express card, the cashier looked at us blankly.

"We don't accept that card."

"That's funny, the sticker on your door says that you do." At this point, I'd been through the drill with numerous failed purchases. Cashiers only knew one type of card, chip & pin, and one way to use it. So, anything without a chip they'd say 'doesn't work.' Even if the logo on the card matched the logo on their terminal, they'd ask for a different card.

Until one day, I asked to inspect the terminal. Wouldn't you know it, I discovered a sliver opening down the right-hand side, just like in the good ol' US of A. I slid my card in the top, magnetic strip facing the machine. Lo and behold the little bugger read it, to the astonishment of the cashier. Bewildered, she handed the receipt and merchandise without asking for a signature. Her other chip & pin transactions never needed a signature, so all transactions must be like that. Since then, I've introduced this magic trick to hundreds of cashiers across the land. I'm Johnny Amex-seed.

Uncurious cashiers are not the only concern. French merchants are six times less likely to accept foreign cards as other European tourist destinations like Spain or Switzerland.

We arrived home too late to rent a video, so we thought we'd watch some public TV. Maybe Zorro would be on. Zorro is always playing on a channel somewhere in France. When I got here, everyone was surprised I'd never heard of the show.

"You don't know Sergeant Garcia? Bernardo? It's an American show, from Disney. Made in the 1950s. It's very popular. You should be familiar because you're from California, where the story takes place. It's all about how California became independent from Spain." From Spain?

I grew up watching six hours of TV a day. Mostly re-runs, a lot of it really old black-and-white stuff like The Little Rascals, the Three Stooges, Shirley Temple. I was not a discerning viewer, and I'd look at any old thing they'd put on. There wasn't a kids' show I hadn't seen. Several times. How this proud icon of Californian programming slipped my young eyes, I do not know.

But the antenna didn't work on our new TV. So we didn't get even a fuzzy channel. Zip, Nada. *No hay Zorro*.

We resigned ourselves to huddling around our son's tiny portable US DVD player, watching Spongebob Squarepants. It was pitiful.

To console themselves, one day my wife and son brought back a new roommate- a cat. I was a bit perturbed, but my son was ecstatic, and so the cat stayed. She became Timinou, which is 3-year-old French for 'little cutie.' I had only one condition and that was she be spayed as soon as possible. The vet told us we would have to wait until she was a couple months older. I'd only ever had male dogs before so I thought, "Well there's probably little risk she'll become pregnant at six months old."

Famous last words.

CHAPTER THREE

Borne 50 - Fait Accompli

Fiat Accompli

I didn't enter the rigmarole of the permit process until the following year. My first year as an expat I didn't bother because I wasn't sure how long I would stay in France. Besides, I knew that initially I could drive legally with my California driver's license. So, I carried my home state license with me when behind the wheel.

We had bought a second-hand Fiat Panda just to have something to putter around from place to place. Where I come from, FIAT stands for 'Fix it again, Tony.' The car was similar in size and shape to a Yugo, with just as much sophistication.

The Fiat Panda was so unremarkable and inadequate in every way, that I re-named it the '*Fait Accompli.*' When I arrived safely at my destination, I'd get out and say 'Ta-da!' ironically, as if I'd successfully completed a harrowing task with bravado.

Like the majority of cars here, the Fiat had a manual transmission. In 2003, 92% of the cars sold in France were manual transmission. That's how my wife learned to drive. People like sticks here because they're €2 000 cheaper to buy and they consume less fuel.

I come from the land of stab and steer, as 90% of all cars in North America have an automatic transmission. Although my first car was a '54 Chevrolet Bel Air with powerglide, I'd been driving stickshifts since my teens.

Driving a manual wasn't difficult, but getting the car in our name *was*. Aurore needed to go to the *Préfecture* four times for a carte grise (the equivalent of a pink slip) for our new/used car. The *Préfecture* is a kind of a neighborhood DMV that also deals with citizenship and other issues. Each time they needed a different piece of paper she wasn't told about on her previous visit. One day, they closed two hours early without advance notice. Just because.

This is par for the course. A fonctionnaire delivering registrations at the *Préfecture* once attributed 16 seats to a Citroën 2CV. That's because the car was listed by the manufacturer as a '4 by 4.'

There was also a trip to the *contrôle technique*. In California, you need to get your car smog-inspected every two years, to make sure it meets emissions standards. However, that's only one part of the French '*contrôle*' or inspection. Here, every two years they test all aspects of the vehicle's road worthiness and safety. Dozens of checks.

Cars in France must carry on them at all times:
- The original *Carte Grise* registration
- a *Contrôle Technique* sticker
- a reflective vest inside the car. If you have to get out to grab the vest from the trunk, it's a violation.
- a reflective triangle in case their car is immobilized
- proof of Insurance, and your insurer's sticker on the windshield
- a breathalyser for your personal use (self-check before taking the wheel). If you've been convicted of drunk driving, you'll have a breathalyser permanently affixed to your vehicle. You must breathe into it and be under the legal alcohol limit, otherwise the car won't start.

In the *contrôle technique*, if any part isn't up to snuff, the car must be repaired immediately before it can go back on the road. Thankfully, the Fait Accompli passed with flying colors. Ta-da!

When it finally arrived, the *carte grise* didn't have my wife's name on it at all, even though she did all the leg-work. Like most things in this patriarchal society, the pink slip was written out to *Monsieur*. It wasn't until 1965 that a French woman had the legal right to accept a job, or open a bank account, or have any property of her own, without her husband's consent. Although nowadays equality is written into the law, certain habits die hard. Whenever we get a letter addressed to both of us, it's written to "*Monsieur et Madame Joe Start.*" *Egalité* my *derrière*.

The day the carte grise arrived, my wife felt like a second-class citizen. We found out later that having *Monsieur* exclusively on the *carte grise* carried some fringe benefits.

The way that traffic tickets and points work in France is like this: moving violations and fines are assigned to the name on the car's registration, *not* to the driver. Each license-holder starts out with 12 points, and with each ticket, points are taken away- one for a small violation, up to six for a DUI. Points are re-instated over time, one for each six months without a ticket. When a driver gets to zero, his license is revoked- and he must start again from scratch.

That's if the driver has a French license. Because I don't have one, no points are taken away from me. Because the car is in my name, ANYONE who drives it is exempt from having points taken away from *them*. Someone would have to pay the fines, but the car could accumulate tickets until the cows came home to Limousin. Fait Accompli!

That following Monday, I began to work in a French company. With more than 50 employees, we had a 'CE' or *'comité d'entreprise'* with many advantages for workers. Rentals of power tools, DVDs, appliances and other items were free. A Normandy cottage could be used over the weekend for a song. Coupons worth $330 of *'chèques cadeaux'* were distributed to employees each summer which could be used to pay for gas, tolls or accomodations on the road to vacation.

There were other benefits, too. My monthly transportation pass on the RER train and bus was only $80. With mandatory 50% employer subventions, the pass became only $40, less than a buck each way. That wouldn't have paid for a week's commute back home in San Francisco.

Lunches were also half-price. Employers must either give coupons, called restaurant tickets, or reduced-price hot meals at a company cafeteria. My company offered the latter, which everybody partook of. Literally, all of my office-mates ate lunch with each other, every single day of the work week. Luckily, they were chatty amongst themselves while I listened and lunched. This precluded me from having to converse much in two languages which I didn't yet master: French, and *femme*.

You see, I was the only man in an office full of women. I was the proverbial *coq* in a *poulailler*. The morning '*bise*' always took about 10 minutes before the two-kiss cheek greeting was completed with my *cohortes*. They all used the '*tu*' form with me, so I didn't have to work on my *vousvoiement*. But, boy did I need a primer on the '*argot*' or slang terms used by *l'autre sexe*. Clothes were '*fringues*.' A child was a '*gamin*' or a '*gosse*.'

I was brought up that terms like 'chick' or 'broad' were derogatory. But these gals freely described themselves, and their female clients in less-than-PC terms. Other women were '*nanas*' at best, '*salopes*' or '*chieuses*' or une '*pétasse poufiasse connasse*' at worst. An expectant mother was a '*pondeuse*' or egg-layer. At any one time, at least two of them were pregnant and teasing each other about it.

Females make up a higher percentage of the workforce in France. Most choose to go right back to work after a five-month paid maternity leave. Toddlers are admitted to nationally-run preschool at two-and-a-half years old. Starting in Primary school, Wednesdays are a half-day for most kids. So, many mothers work what's called *4/5ème*- longer hours Monday-Tuesday and Thursday-Friday so they can stay home Wednesday. At least three of my colleagues worked at this rhythm.

My wife worked a full-day Wednesday, so I was tasked with shuttling sonny from pre-school to soccer practice. Driving to pick him up, I passed by one of those ubiquitous 'school zone' signs, this one saying 'Attention 200 students.' Every school sign is strangely customized for the number of kids at that establishment, so you'll see 'Attention 300 students,' or 'Attention 700 students,' etc. as if people will be more careful because there are more children. Pity the school with only 50 students, as the drivers lay a drag strip in front.

Aurore could pick him up when the two-hour practice session was over. Sébastien's home-taught French vocabulary was soon spiced up by the salty locker-room banter of his soccer coach. Hopping in the car after training one day, he instructed Aurore to "*roule ma poule*," essentially "step on it, chickie!"

The handoff was necessary because my office hours didn't end until 7 p.m., which is pretty normal for France. Although the law is a 35-hour workweek, almost everyone clocks 40 or more. The 'excess' is counted toward more days off, known as 'RTT' for '*réduction de temps du travail*.' I got 20 RTT days in addition to the 25 vacation days required by law. This gave me nine weeks' paid time off, not including public holidays. When I worked in the 'States, I clocked 300 more hours per year than the average French employee. More than half of all US employees don't use all their vacation days, just giving them up. Working in France was more like the work/life balance I was looking for.

The estrogen level wasn't the only *différence* in the *bureau*. My keyboard didn't have the familiar Q-W-E-R-T-Y letters in the upper-left-hand corner. Instead it read 'A-Z-E-

R-T-Y' The letters Q and Z are so prevalent they're worth nothing in French scrabble. So, their placement on the keyboard was swapped with the A and W, respectively. The M was also moved, along with other characters popular in English. Maybe the inventor was trying to avoid being labeled a 'bqstqrd son of q zhore.'

On the AZERTY keyboard, you must hold the shift key for characters you use all the time, like numbers '0123456789,' or the period '.' at the end of every sentence. If the extra keystroke increases your frustration by 98.76% making you shout '*#?&!' you'll have to shift to type all of those numbers and symbols, too. They even have a special shift button which doesn't exist on the Qwerty, the '*alt gr*' to activate the '@' symbol, if you can find it on the Azerty keyboard. Website addresses with w's, dots and forward slashes are a particular joy. What's baffling is that characters you hardly ever use, like ';' semicolon, '^' hat, '`' backwards apostrophe and '§' squiggle don't require the shift key.

I was a pretty quick typist before dropping to five words per minute in my new environment. I felt like Art Tatum being handed an accordion to play. Eventually, a guy from IT showed me a trick on the operating system to toggle between the two. Everything was fine as long as I didn't look down at the keys.

When I wasn't in front of the computer, I was travelling to meet with clients. I also had client visits back in the 'States, but this time it was travel to exotic foreign lands. Instead of Dallas, Denver, Detroit, it was Madrid, Milan, Munich. I visited 12 countries in one year. Germans, Dutch, Swiss and Swedes all bought from me.

It was so satisfying to reach agreements across borders, cultures and languages. Clients were numerous, content and loyal. I was living the European dream, travelling without a passport across the EU, transacting in a common currency which was only two years old.

Returning to Paris, the familiar but still unwelcoming terrain shocked my system. French freeways routinely closed at night for road works with no warning, and no detour signs suggesting alternate routes.

My superiors always tempered my enthusiasm as well. It's really a different relationship between bosses and employees in France. It's as if the monarchy slunk back after the Revolution. Only 42% of French workers have confidence in their bosses. And 36% of employees don't feel that their French hierarchy respects them. I was accepted everywhere but Paris. One day, walking in the parking lot, the HR director almost ran me over. He sped by without stopping or even acknowledging me.

The song about New York says that if you can make it there, you can make it anywhere. The songsmith didn't know what the hell he was talking about. New York is a cakewalk compared to Paris.

However, my new life was so rich, the culture, the cuisine, the time off to explore all these distinctive regions. I wanted to make it here. I wanted to stay.

I came home from work one day to find our little family had grown. Five newborn kittens had oozed out from their mother onto the coat I'd left on the bed. Thanks, Timinou!

These were the many little signs that my expat experience might last longer than a year. My day of reckoning with the permit people was nigh.

CHAPTER FOUR

Borne 75 - Discovering French road idiotsyncrasies

A la découverte des idiotsynchracies des routes françaises

I landed in France before GPS devices became common. So, I had to rely on old-fashioned paper maps and road signs to guide me.

Using this method, the first thing I discovered is that I will not be told by French road signs which cardinal direction I am going in, either north south east or west. I will not be given an indication of the next big city. Nor will I be informed how far away that city is.

Instead, I will be told where the very next small to medium-sized village or town is on my path. That's it, one village. So, setting a course for a larger city involves plotting out about a dozen small towns along the way and aiming for those in precise order. This involves a lot of stopping and re-verifying your list unless you have a co-pilot.

Sometimes you are offered two options to get to the same place. 'For Le Pecq, stay in the left lane, but if you'd prefer to go to Le Pecq, by all means stay in the right lane.' This can happen in towns when you're coming to a roundabout. The right lane remains at street level and feeds into the roundabout. The left lane goes into an underground tunnel, and comes out on the other side flowing down the same road after the tunnel/roundabout.

French roads are broken up into regular streets, Départemental roads labeled 'D' shown with white signs, Nationale roads 'N' on green signs and Autoroutes or freeways 'A' on blue signs. Autoroutes are few and far between. Only 1% of French roads are Autoroutes. Europe's freeways were laid long after the cities and villages sprung up, so, the autoroutes are way out in the country where no one lives. Often you have to go well out of your way to get on one, and then, the trajectory is not always ideal. There are far fewer exits, commonly one every 10 miles or more. You end up getting off well-before, or well-after your destination, and taking a D or an N anyway. Apart from long-haul, almost all driving is done on these smaller roads.

Many roads fill up routinely, because driving dozens of extra miles to a freeway is even worse. Congestion concentrates regularly on certain Nationales, such as the N10 around Trappes or the N184 near Conflans-Sainte-Honorine. The obvious solution would be to modify the Nationales, which are overused, and turn them into

Autoroutes, fluidifying the circulation. However, there's strong local opposition to this. Residents host loud protests, post banners on overpasses and sometimes build human chains across the road.

When your trip on one of these secondary roads takes you through a strange town and you're unsure where to turn next, there's a helpful sign that will inevitably turn up, indicating '*TOUTES DIRECTIONS*.' This means '**all directions**.' "Nothing to see here. Just pass through. I don't care where you're going to, it's obviously this way." So, you comply and, sure enough, a bit farther up the road, your next waypoint is clearly marked, and you breeze along, confident you will arrive at your destination.

Until you once again come across the now-familiar '*TOUTES DIRECTIONS*' arrow, pointing to the right. You're about to head that way when you notice another sign just next to it, labeled '*AUTRES DIRECTIONS*' pointing to the left. This, of course, means '**other directions**.' How, you ponder, does '**all**' differ from '**other**?'

Being well-schooled in philosophy, the French driver in front of you speeds on. Scratching your Yankee head, you pull to the side of the road and wait for the mass-market adoption of GPS.

Or, you do eenie-meenie-minee-moe and hope for the best.

I had one of those life-changing decisions offered to me early on in my French driving adventure. We needed housewares for our new place, so we headed out one Saturday afternoon to Conforama, an equivalent of Kmart. On the way there, I spotted a Midas. Our Fiat sounded a bit gassy, and I saw this as an opportunity to kill two birds with one stone.

"Hey honey," I said, "how about I drop you off at Conforama, while I double-back to Midas to check out the exhaust? It's only five minutes away, on the other side of this same road, so I'll be back here in no time." She agreed, exiting the car fully confident in my sense of direction, forgetting this wasn't my country.

I made the first turn easy enough, re-tracing our tracks. The road we had come through contained slower traffic on the right, at ground-level, where you could see the shops, and faster traffic on the left speeding straight ahead through an underground tunnel to destinations beyond the commercial area. I wasn't going to miss the entrance to the Midas at street-level, so I stayed right. Too right.

This turned out to be the onramp to an Autoroute. I hadn't seen the second bifurcation. You were supposed to merge right then immediately left to the beginning of a roundabout if you wanted to continue on the same road.

I felt like a dope, but stayed the course without resorting to a radical lane change to the left. I figured there would be another offramp coming up soon enough that would allow me to correct my mistake. The trees waved by and the kilometers piled up as I waited for a road sign to indicate my next possibility for escape.

And waited.

And waited.

10 miles of unfriendly asphalt rolled by like this. Still there was no offramp nor any indication of one coming up. The dash clock turned and turned. I began to take account of the gravity of my error and was no longer seeking to return to Midas. I would be happy just to return to my wife at Conforama.

As this much humbler wish crossed my mind a road

sign appeared. Surely I was to be rewarded for my newfound humility. It was another five miles before I could take that opportunity and leave this freeway. Merging from the motorway in a determined fashion, I entered... another freeway.

This new freeway was six lanes wide, twice as big as the one I just left. The awesome autoroute stretched out far into the distance with no end in sight.

I was inconsolable, which was just as well because there was no one around to console me. Not only will I fail my mission, but I'm likely to strand my beloved for a long time. Maybe I'd never return.

My thoughts turned to Homer. How long was Odysseus away from Penelope? Two decades? He must've come up with some whopper of an excuse.

My next move, 20 miles hence actually proved to be a prudent one. I was able to retrace my route without further error. It took me 30 more minutes to make my way back. That gave me time to come up with a story that was believable: I bungled.

I pulled into the parking lot which I had started out from an hour earlier. The lot was now in shadows and desolate, near closing time. Outside the store my wife was standing with two heavy bags at her sides.

"Where the hell have you been?"

I sheepishly began my prepared explanation, but there was no time to finish. We desperately needed closet space, and this being Saturday, it was the only day to shop together. The stores were all closed Sunday. It was also early evening, so we'd have to rush to make it to But.

You read that right, 'But.' That's the name of the store, pronounced like the English 'boot,' which is what my wife gave me as she took the wheel.

CHAPTER FIVE

Borne 100 - The Customer is always wrong

Le client a toujours tort

As an American, it's considered our constitutionally protected right to be treated well when we're the ones paying. We want what we want, impeccably and immediately. We have no obligation of courtesy to those who serve us. It's the American way dolgarnnit, and our God-given privilege.

In my family, we exercise this birthright to extremes. My relatives have been known to buy expensive rugs, tread on them for five years and return them successfully for the original price. They've bought an item on discount at store A, and returned it for a full-price refund at store B. They work the system.

This is completely foreign to my wife, Aurore. Raised in France, she's used to bagging her own groceries, taking a day off to wait for the phone repairman, and paying 35 centimes per minute charges while on hold waiting to speak to support. Toll-free numbers in France are almost unheard of. Returns can be a hassle, even when you *do* have the receipt. For large items it's common to pay in full upfront at the time of ordering, then wait months for delivery. Hygena had our €700 cash for five months before our bathroom sink and cupboards arrived. We had no recourse.

Aurore expatriated to the San Francisco Bay area, where we eventually met. She hardly knew a soul there. So, she was surprised and delighted with the friendly welcome she received at Safeway.

"How are you today, Rorrora? OK if I pack your groceries in plastic, Miss Camarama? I'll double-bag the Ben & Jerry's to keep it colder Arorey. Would you like me to carry those to your car, Miss Creameralla?"

It didn't matter to her that they always butchered her name. The same cashier usually mispronounced two different ways, two days in a row, without genuinely recognizing her. Employees were trained to do that, like robots, and they could be fired for NOT doing it. She didn't care, said mechanically or not, it was a sign to her that she was valued and less alone in the world.

When consumers in America don't get our way, we very confidently play our trump card. Ask to speak to the manager.

In France, this method can backfire. An American *tourist was denied access* to a floor of the Eiffel Tower because she didn't have the right ticket. She was told to go back down and buy a new one. She refused, was removed from the elevator, and then complained to a manager. This being one of the top tourist attractions in the world, the management said they would accommodate her. This being France, all of the elevator operators and staff immediately went on strike, backing their co-worker, who had followed procedure. For two days, NOBODY could ride up the Eiffel Tower.

I was aware of the reputation, but didn't expect the way customer service backfired on me.

We needed an armoire for our son's clothes. Like most living spaces here, the lovely, ornate façade of our *maison de gardien* belied the sparsely furnished interior. There are very few requirements put on landlords beyond supplying heat and water. Cheap tile, paper-thin carpet, and bare bulbs hanging without fixtures are par for the course. Landlords aren't required to provide a refrigerator nor a way to cook food, nor a dishwasher to clean up after. Unfurnished means exactly that- not one speck of furniture, no appliances, no storage whatsoever outside the kitchen. Of course there were no closets.

But (the store) sold the kind of armoire we were looking for, but didn't have it in stock. It needed to be ordered. We did so, and paid in full upfront. A week later we were wondering if we'd taken too big a risk, because it still hadn't arrived. Finally, we got the call that the armoire was ready. Over the phone the guy couldn't reliably explain how big the box was. I decided to have a look, driving the Fait Accompli back out there, 30 miles away, by myself like a big boy. After living here for a month or so, I was feeling more confident about my sense of direction and rudimentary French.

I went to the pickup point and there were no customers in front of me. Goodie. I showed my papers to see the box. It took about 10 minutes to be pushed out on a cart. One look told me it would not fit in the car. I explained my predicament to the guy, pointing to the Fiat, which he could clearly see through the window as the only car in the lot.

"The box won't fit in that car," he stated factually.

"Yes, that's clear," I adopted an exasperated tone. "But what other options can you provide? Do you have any rental vans, for example?"

"There's that one." He indicated an enormous truck, enough to move an entire house in one trip.

"I don't need something so big. Don't you have anything else?"

"They're all out."

"I can see that, but when will they return?"

"Which size truck?"

"How do I know?" I huffed. "Will the box fit in your smallest van?"

"Yes." He waited. Didn't he see where this was going? Couldn't he anticipate my next question?

"Well, when will your smallest van come back?"

He tap-tapped on his terminal. "Monday."

"That's not going to work for me, obviously." My eyes widened. "I live far from here and I work Monday. Do you have any other transportation vehicles coming back today."

He looks at his monitor. "Yes."

"Are you going to tell me which size and when?"

Tappy tappy. "One with 30 cubic meters of

capacity will be back at 18 hours."

"That's a couple hours from now, hmmm, OK, how much does that one cost?"

"It's €16 per hour, plus fuel, and you need to return it a half-hour before we close."

"When do you close?"

"19 hours."

Fast breath exited my nose and my mouth clenched sideways. "I can't very well make the trip to my home far away and back in 30 minutes, you know that." It was about to get personal, and I knew that wasn't the way to get what I wanted.

"How much for the enormous truck then?"

"Let me check, uh, in the back..." and he exited behind the long plastic strips that served as the door to the warehouse. He left me there to stew for at least 10 minutes.

When a comprehension barrier emerges in a foreign country and you're not getting what you want from a customer service rep, you have no idea why. Is my request unclear? Am I asking the wrong person? Is this simply not done here? Is the representative having a bad day? Does this person hate foreigners? Are they incompetent? Are they a malicious jerk? Are they a student scientist who took a service job as part of Mantes La Jolie University sociology department's study of human behavior under stress? Have I just walked into an immersive performance art show demonstrating the brutality of our consumer society?

In your own culture, you'd know instinctively what the hang-up was, and you'd act on your sixth sense. You wouldn't wait around like me, trying to teach a pig to sing the answer to my problem. My lack of cultural knowledge left me dumbfounded, without a solution in view.

I remained alone and confused, without another client or employee around to commiserate with in that big, bare room. My glazed-over eyes finally focused on a legal-looking black-and-white paper displayed on the counter right in front of me. 'Ask us about delivery,' it read, with several accompanying paragraphs of terms and conditions. I resolved to do just that when he returned.

"It says here that you deliver," I mentioned, hopefully.

"Yes, that's correct." Zero change in expression. No acknowledgement that this was an option he could have mentioned at the start. Delivery was simply another outlandish idea that had been filed away in his brain. Delivery swam around in his cerebellum with other theoretical possibilities, like a flock of radio-controlled geese flying with strings attached to the box below.

"Well, then, how much would delivery cost?"

Tappy tappy tappy. "At the price you paid for your item, delivery is... free."

I did a double-take. Maybe it was a triple-take. Elmer Fudd would have given me props.

Did two somewhat educated human beings really spend the last 20 minutes searching so desperately for such a simple solution? Was it really right in front of our noses the whole time?

Excitedly now. "Whhell, when can you deliver the armoire?"

"Monday."

With customer service agents in France, you really need to know to ask precisely the right question.

CHAPTER SIX

Borne 125 - Bike Follies I

Vélo en folie

When we first arrived, we just had the one car. My wife used the Fait Accompli to get to and from work, while I used public transportation.

While I really liked the public options in our former little corner of the Bay Area, it doesn't come close to the transportation system they have in Paris. For example, take connections, or *correspondances*, as the French call them. BART, the equivalent of the Parisian RER, only intersects the local San Francisco Muni, or *métro* at four stations. The cable cars, nowadays impractical for all but tourists, only intersect at two BART stations. The transbay bus terminal is connected to zero stations- no BART, no Muni no Cable Car. The light rail station coming up from the Peninsula doesn't connect to BART nor the bus terminal, and is at least a 10 minute walk to Market Street and the beginning of the city center. As a result, San Francisco commuters avoid transfers. They're more trouble than they're worth. When I worked there, I remember preferring a 20-minute walk from the bus terminal to offices near Pier 39 over any alternatives, even in pouring January rain.

Within Paris intramuros, you're never farther than a 300 meter walk from a Métro station. This makes Paris the best connected city for public transportation in the world. Connection options abound, with suburban rail, buses, trams, and even public bikes. The capacity the system can handle is amazing. There are 1.2 million passengers who ride the A line of the RER daily. That's more than the entire population of the city of San Francisco- on one Paris train line.

Who pays for all this infrastructure? Well, 80% of riders contribute. However, 20% of them don't. Rampant fraud is an enormous issue, adding up to an astonishing €366 million in lost revenue annually. You routinely see people of all ages and backgrounds jumping the turnstiles, often aided by paying customers who hold the barrier open for following *fraudeurs*. A recent operation by 500 agents at the Gare du Nord recorded an astonishing 1 493 fines in only three hours.

I often wondered if turnstile jumpers were motivated more by the excitement of breaking the law, than the savings. Because it's hard to beat the very affordable Parisian transportation system. Even today, a single ticket to go from point-to-point anywhere in Paris costs only €1.90 or

$2.04. A monthly Navigo card granting unlimited rides throughout all 5 zones is only €73 ($80). The equivalent Oyster card pass in London will set you back $445.

When I wasn't on the train, I'd explore our surroundings by foot or by bike. We were lucky to have found a home in such a green area, with much history. There were many riverside paths, nearby forests and woods, all within five miles or a one-stop train ride. I visited the fascinating engineering works of old pumps carrying water from the Seine up the hill in Le Port Marly and over an aqueduct to the fountains at Versailles seven miles away. There was the *Château of Saint-Germain-en-Laye* where Louis XIV was born. And there was the Île des Impressionists in Chatou where Renoir's 'Garden Party' is set.

We went there one day to visit the Maison Fournaise, which was the scene of the *'Dejeuner des canotiers'* painting. The Maison was closed, but the staff was kind enough to let us visit the spot from which Renoir painted.

Just opposite the bridge, on the other side of the island, there was a big crowd, so we went to check it out. It turned out to be the 80th annual Festival of *Antiques and Ham*. There were chamber pots... and *charcuterie*. Sculptures and *salami*. Ceramics and cured ham. What a pairing. Nobody could explain what these things had in common, nor why they put them together at the same event. Maybe it was process of elimination. They certainly attracted more WASPs and *Cathos* than Israelites and *Maghrébans*. We bought some *jambon* and left without any antiques.

When we first moved to the other side of the Atlantic, we had received many hand-me-downs from relatives, including an older basic bicycle my wife got from her sister.

One day, I wanted to have a little exercise on the yellow bike by going to return a video. I thought I'd also pump up her back tire, which was only about half full with air. I knew how to get to a local service station. It was in the opposite direction from the video place. I didn't mind that the Total station about was two kilometers away, because I wanted to exercise. That I did, pushing the pedals that resisted turning that under-inflated tire. Huffing was only slightly faster than walking.

When I got to the Total station, I took off the plastic covers and noticed the valve on the back tire was different from the front tire. It was also unlike anything I'd seen before. I tried many different ways to make the pump fit the contraption, without success, each time, letting a little more air out of the tire against my will. Finally, I hooked it in a certain way that seemed to be working more than the other ways, because it made a different whooshing noise. I saw too late that the back tire was now completely flat.

Asking the guy inside, he said he didn't know anything about bikes, but I might try the Esso gas station down the road, 500 yards farther from home. I did, and it was closed. Then, I saw another one, an Elf, in the distance, about another 500 yards, again farther from home. The Elf was open, but the guy there told me he couldn't help because he didn't have a '*tige*.'

This is when you realize you're getting pretty good at a language. When you can understand 90% of what people say to you. That's also when it becomes dangerous.

Imagine you've rented a Paris apartment for the weekend, and the owner's giving you a walk-through. You're so proud of yourself because you've navigated this far, finding the address, agreeing on price and dates, and the place is exactly like you wanted. Just before leaving, she says "Oh and one more thing- on the pipe to the left of the toilet, don't touch the '*poignée du robinet*' or it may cause a '*fuite*.' Ciao, ciao." The door shuts. "Poynyay doo robinay? Fweete?" Panicked, you spend the next three days without flushing.

What the hell was a '*tige*?' I wondered. The Elf service station cashier said that the Total I just came from should have one. Walking my bike back, I encountered the Total dude again, who said that if he had had a *tige*, he wouldn't have sent me down the road in the first place.

I got my exercise pushing the bike two kilometers back home. My bike fun was done, but the video was still in my sack.

I drove the Fiat to the video shop. The door was locked, so I slipped the movie through the slot. It landed among dozens strewn about the floor. The walls were bare and no one was inside. Strange for a Saturday afternoon. It then dawned on me that they were out of business. I remembered the last time I was there, the owner offered me an incredible €2 per movie rental price if I paid €50 upfront. This day was designed to make me feel like a dope.

At Decathlon, I finally got my '*tige*' in the form of a two-headed pump, one side for the world I come from, and one side from Bizzarroworld. I affixed the pump to the bike for just such a future emergency.

CHAPTER SEVEN

Borne 150 - Car Culture

La culture de la caisse

California has a strong car culture. Shrines abound to venerate the vehicle. Southern Cal is home to the Petersen automotive museum and Northern Cal has the Blackhawk Auto Museum. Most of America identifies itself as a car-loving people. Our cars help define who we are, our personality, our status.

TV Shows from Car 54, Where are you? to Route 66, to Taxi, to Night Rider have filled our screens for decades. Even today, the shows roll at all hours of the day. Top Gear. Pimp My Ride. James Corden carpool karaoke. Jerry Seinfeld's Comedians in Cars Getting Coffee.

There are miles and miles of film running US car Movies. Remember Thunder Road? Herbie, the Love Bug? How 'bout American Graffiti? Or Christine? You could have seen any of these at a drive-in theater, another invention right out of the US of A. The hit parade continues with modern flicks Drive, Rush, Cars 1, 2 and 3, Fast and Furious 1 through freakin' 8. Baby Driver. The opening scene in LA LA Land.

There's even a sister site to IMDB.com called 'IMCDB.org' listing makes and models in movies. There, I learned that 'Two for the Road' takes place in France, but the main character is the Brit Albert Finney rolling around in a right-drive Triumph, directed by American Stanley Donan.

An endless long playlist of hit Music from America lauding cars sings through the ages... Maybelline. Bo Diddley's 'Cadillac.' Bruce Springsteen's 'Pink Cadillac.' Janis Joplin's 'Mercedes Benz.' My Woody. Cruising. Hot Rod Lincoln. Free Ride. Car Wash. I Can't Drive 55.

Your local US radio station will play these car hits in-between traffic updates. KNX in LA reports Sigalerts every 10 minutes. Not once have any of them helped me avoid congestion. The most helpful and humorous auto-themed radio program was Car Talk with Tom and Ray which ran on NPR for more than 20 years.

Countless English-language expressions used in America allude to the automobile in non-driving situations: hit the gas, floor it, running on empty, out of gas, my way or the highway, hit the road, pedal to the metal, take me for a ride, middle of the road, get the show on the road, asleep at the wheel, fifth wheel, and then the wheels fell off. They're all heard commonly in the US, and have been for years.

Not surprisingly, the US is in the top two of car-owning countries in the world, with 755 cars per 1000 residents and an amazing 1.26 cars on the road for every licensed driver. More than 17 Million new cars were sold in the US in 2015. Although they only have 25 million cars today, the Chinese would become the drivingest folks on the planet if their government would let them. Millions of people in China can now afford new cars. Thankfully, to prevent pollution getting worse, big cities severely restrict car ownership. Beijing has a license-plate lottery, and only $1/10^{th}$ of 1% of applicants win a plate. However, if a man has one, he can transfer his rights to his wife. So, folks in Beijing are arranging false 'green card' marriages, just to get the right to drive. They still have to pay a year's salary for the privilege. When they win the right to buy, more and more go electric, at a rate far greater than the US. In 2016, 320 000 electric vehicles were sold in China, versus 159 000 in America.

Portugal just edges out the USA for the top spot at 778 cars per capita. That's likely due to their relatively low population, limited public transportation, and the fact that Portugal is a major country for building cars. Manufacturers from France and Spain farm out a lot of their production to Portugal.

On a trip to Spain to visit a former roommate, he took me to a paella party some friends of his were throwing in the suburbs of Madrid. I remember one guy staring at me pretty intently, but not engaging me in conversation. I thought he wanted to speak to the foreigner, but didn't know English. Finally, several *cerveza* later, he overcame his shyness.

"Excuse me, Joe, but can I ask you a very personal

question?"

"Um, uhhhh sure."

"Is it true that Americans eat in their cars?"

He couldn't fathom it. It was so removed from his culture. To him, and most Europeans, a meal is a conversation, something shared. Food is always served when a group is around a table, talking and eating. Adding any other activity to the mix like TV or walking or a board game or driving, ruins the whole experience for Europeans.

Another time, in France, a co-worker asked what I was doing for lunch. "I've got a conference call in a half hour, so I'm just going to grab a sandwich quickly. Would you like to come with me?"

"Oh, no. I always have a sit-down lunch, with a hot meal. Whenever I have a sandwich, I feel like I'm being punished."

Americans consider their cars to be extensions of their living space. Of course we eat in our cars. What else are the eight cup holders for? We also put on makeup, shave, fix our hair and put on earrings- all activities I've personally seen from my fellow drivers while in motion on a California commute. Some of us Americans have been conceived and born in back seats.

You need room for all of these activities, so Americans invented the SUV. Sport-utility vehicles now represent 39% of all new cars sold in our great country. The Hummer, an abomination on civilian roadways, is a uniquely American invention. We like our cars big, and we like them new.

I've lost that loving feeling for cars. I must have had it at some point. I delivered pizzas in my '54 Chevy as a teen. I loved to be alone with my thoughts and my tunes. In college, I washed UPS trucks. There was an incline in the back where we'd park to let the water and suds wash out. On my last day, we took one of the vans out back and got air on that jump! The car was a ticket to joy back in those days.

Both uncles on my Mom's side were paid to race cars and anything else they could sit their leathers on. Speedway bikes without any brakes. Stock cars they'd race in figure 8 banger style. Demolition derby in my parents' used 1970s Chevy station wagon.

My Father wants me paternity-tested to see if he really has a son who's so ambivalent about autos. He grew up fixing cars, put together a motorcycle from scratch, and got his first job at the Chevy plant in Detroit. When I was in high school, my rear differential needed a rebuild. I slyly suggested we do it together. Dad jumped at the chance for a father-son project. After 15 minutes, I went inside for a 'drink' and didn't return until the work was finished.

These days, I can't wait for the ride to be over.

The French attitude toward cars mirrors my current state. There are no popular songs or shows or movies about cars in France. This, despite the fact that we can credit the French for foundational contributions. The brand Cadillac was named after the founder of Detroit, a Frenchman named Antoine de la Mothe Cadillac. In 1903, 49% of the world's car production was from French manufacturers. Then Henry Ford came along, and in 20 years, owned 50% market share globally.

There are very few French expressions on the topic, and the ones which do exist are from like 100 years ago.

They say '*attention au retour de manivelle*' to mean 'warning, your effort could backfire.' The *manivelle* is the hand-crank needed to start the Model-T Ford and contemporary vehicles from the beginning of the 20th century. Our 'step on the gas' is said '*appuyer sur le champignon*' because the shape of the accelerator way back when was a metal knob which looked like a mushroom.

There are more French songs and films about bicycles than about the automobile. Yves Montand's '*A bicyclette,*' and movies, like '*Les triplettes de Belleville*' come to mind. Charles Trenet did have a hit with '*Rn7,*' but that song was much more about the destination- vacation in the South of France- than the journey on the Nationale 7 before the advent of the Autoroutes.

Well, I must admit there were three car-related French songs, all rather unlistenable, and only one successful. Claude François danced on hoods and trunks for his TV introduction of '*Ma nouvelle voiture*' which hardly got any airplay in 1963 and thankfully disappeared quickly. A few years later in 1967, Serge Gainsbourg sang about a car, but not a French model- a Ford Mustang on an album named for a French model, Brigitte Bardot. It's not really about a car, like most Gainsbourg, the lyrics are not really about anything. The car is just one of several objects named haphazardly, unemotionally, understately and without much interest.

Vanessa Paradis had a hit in 1988 with 'Joe le Taxi,' albeit not a song about a personal vehicle. But I'll bet the popularity of *Mademoiselle Paradis'* tube had more to do with the fact that she was 14 at the time, whispering through her 'lucky teeth' in a naïve and alluring fashion about being driven alone by a black man. "*Vas-y, Joe, fonce!*" she sang, encouraging her man to "Go ahead, Joe, lay into it!" Since 1945, the age of consent in France has been set at 15 years old. For Joe the taxi to avoid being arrested, he must've kept his hands on the wheel for a year. Some fare.

There are more movies about underground rail than about the voiture, like '*Le dernier métro*,' or '*Zazie dans le métro.*' The Transporter, from Luc Besson's production company, is somewhat French. But the cars are not. *Mon dieu*, the lead actor, Jason Statham is *English*, of all things!

The best French car film wasn't made for public screening. Claude Lelouch shot an underground short in 1976 crossing Paris in his Mercedes without stopping for nine minutes called "*C'était un rendez-vous*" Adrenalin rush is assured because it's *all* real, and *all illegal*. Speed limits are blown away, red lights run, one-way streets reversed, blind alleys crossed, and many, many close calls with other drivers and pedestrians are seen. All 12 points of moving violations are spent before the end of the first minute. Then it gets worse.

Have you ever heard of Sebastien Loeb? No? How about Jeff Gordon? Yes? That's because auto racing is popular in America, and many of its best drivers are American. Our tracks are nearly all oval-shaped and closed-circuit with controlled conditions and special surfaces specifically designed for racing. Personally, I don't see the point of go fast, turn left, go fast, turn left in NASCAR. I'd attribute the differences in placement at the finish line more to the machines than the skills of the pilots. I'm perhaps in the minority among Americans. An incredible number of my countrymen are huge fans of stock car racing.

The French prefer reckless adventure to the strict rules of track racing. Professional driver Sebastien Loeb races Rallye cars through dirt and mud on crazy turns in the middle of nowhere. Thin ropes separate viewers and livestock from the often out-of-control cars, and collisions are common. The Paris, France to Dakar, Senegal rally used to race up to 600 motorcycles and all-terrain vehicles through mountains, desert and jungle. Now, it's just called the 'Dakar' and less than 100 vehicles participate, mostly amateurs. Today, the race is held in South America, of all places.

"What about the 24 Hours of Le Mans?" you may say. "Or the Grand Prix of Monaco?" Well, first of all, Monaco is a different country. Secondly, these events are parties that are thrown for visitors from out of town. The majority of spectators, participants and auto manufacturers travel from across France's borders to participate. Of the 49 cars which participated in the 1971 Monaco Grand Prix, 67% were Porsches. The last time a French driver won there was 20 years ago.

I've never come across anybody in France who has mentioned attending, watching or caring about these races, considered two of the 'triple crown' of racing among autosport fans globally, along with the Indianapolis 500. All this time, I've lived only two hours away from Le Mans. Can you imagine anyone living within commuting distance of Indianapolis who's never been there for race week? More than 400 000 people buy tickets to the Indianapolis 500. The entire population of Monaco is only 38 000 people.

There was one French racer of note in this year's Le Mans. His name is Thomas Laurent, and at 19 years old, he became a member of Jackie Chan DC Racing, which won in their LMP2 category. Even he admitted that he rarely watched Formula One, because it's *'chiant'* or 'boring as hell.' "The guy who starts in pole position finishes first eight times out of 10 and doesn't really have any course management to speak of." What does he prefer? *Karting*, or go-karts, where he's won the world championship already several times over at his young age.

It's true, riding go-karts in France is a rare thrill. There are more than 300 tracks throughout the country. Karts used by the general public have no seatbelts, and can go from zero to 100 km/h in three seconds. 13-year-olds are allowed to drive the adult versions which can easily surpass the equivalent California freeway speed limit of 65-70 mph.

Even though major auto racing events did originate in France, there isn't much enthusiasm among today's French population to follow these races, watch on TV or attend in-person. The events might get a page in the national sports newspaper *L'Equipe* from time to time, which pales in comparison to the voracious coverage in the British, German or Italian media. Formula One, on regular city surface streets is the most popular form of auto racing. However, it's considered an elitist sport, for the one-per-centers, and again, followed much more by France's neighbors than the French. There hasn't been a Formula One race in France for 10 years.

Paris is the site of the *Mondial de l'Automobile* or Paris Motor Show each October. It's one of the biggest showcases for auto builders, but still about half the size of the Frankfurt auto show, which welcomes 930 000 people. For the *Mondial* most visitors and exhibitors are from outside France. The hosts don't much go to the *Mondial* to buy a car. Again, France throws a great party, but she's rarely the belle of the auto ball.

Only 83% of French households have a car. Of those, half own just one car. So, it's multiple-car owners which push up the number of personal cars on the road. There's an association called "*40 millions d'automobilistes*" or "40 Million Drivers" in France, which sounds like a lot. But they should change their name- there are only 32 million car owners. Compared to the population of 64 million, it's relatively low for a Western nation. Several million drive their employer's car, or their spouse's. For the 2nd most populous country in Europe, France only comes in at #4 for new car sales on the continent.

When shopping for a car, the French consumer doesn't play favorites. There's no equivalent of the Ford vs. Chevy debate, pitting passionate advocates on both sides. Chevrolet isn't even sold in France anymore. Only 34% of French consumers are loyal to their brand when purchasing a new car. This indifference leaves the market wide open for dozens of brands. Diversity on French roads is widespread- many more brands than are sold in the 'States. You won't see any of these on US roads: Lancia, Skoda, Loda, Opel, Vauxhall, Seat, Dacia, Logan, Bolloré or Ssanyong. Protectionist policies are a major reason why the US car market is so homogenous.

However, nearly all brands sold in America are *also* sold in France. This may surprise US consumers because they never see French cars. The three French brands (Peugeot, Citroen, Renault) and all but the highest-end Italian brands (Ferrari, Lamborghini, Maserati) left the American market several decades ago. The Renault R5 '*Le Car*' only sold in the tens of thousands in the US between 1976 and 1982 and *zero* of those sales happened in California. Fiat only came back with the acquisition of

Chrysler in 2014. Alfa Romeo announced their return to America with a 2017 Super Bowl spot. The Smart car was only recently introduced to the US. It's not likely they will stick around. Smart, designed by Swatch, never sold more than 120 000 units a year in Europe. The ride is very shaky above 45mph, so most people don't take them on the freeway, which is a must in the US.

Rural dwellers in France also push up the number of car owners, as 93% of people who live in a town with less than 20 000 people own a car. If they could do without, many of them would. Only 62% of Parisian-area residents own a car. Even this is deceiving. There are many communes with less than 20 000 residents that have direct train service to Paris in less than an hour. Ile-de-France includes the *départements* of the Yvelines and Seine-et-Marne which have much more farm land than towns. Trains in the Paris region have been blocked by sheep and other livestock getting out over the tracks.

Of car owners, only 71% use their cars daily. If it's for a short trip, they'll often walk or bike, for 42% of trips under one kilometer the French don't use a car. Whether using a car or public transportation, the French don't commute far. The average is only 25 minutes one way from home to work, or work to home. Even in the UK, the average one-way commute is only 31 minutes.

People in France keep their cars longer. The average age of a car in France is 8 1/2 years old. This has actually grown over time. In 1980, the average car was six years old. There are three times as many used cars as new cars on the French roads, and that trend will increase. There are three times more used cars purchased than new in France, helped by services like Carizy. In 1980, the figure was two times as many used cars versus new on French roads.

French cars are kept, but not well-kept. They're washed once per year, if at all. They're parked on the street, even in the rare case when owners have a garage. Better to use the garage for storage than their unloved *bagnole*. Car covers are non-existant. Bumper stickers? Personalization is an afterthought. Vanity license plates are forbidden. Bright colors, shiny rims and custom accessories are nowhere to be found.

Only for weddings are cars dressed up with ribbons. You see them in October, with tattered brown lace still dangling precariously from broken sideview mirrors and cracked bumpers, a relic of the June ceremony, the last time their car touched soap.

People who are well-off in France own cars because it's easier than the alternative, and they can afford the expenses. The average car owner in France, owns one because he has to. The car is just a €6 000 a year burden that he must put up with, and he tries to control fees as best he can. Car expenses are 15% of the average French person's budget. Think about that. Their first two months' wages are consumed in paying for their car.

The cost of car ownership, especially in France, is more and more out of control. Today, between driver training, auto purchase taxes, customs, fuel taxes, tolls, fines, registration and renewal fees, the French state pockets more than €60 Billion annually from drivers. Half of that comes from gas and diesel taxes alone, 66% of the cost of a fillup. If taxes weren't assessed, fuel would be cheaper in France than in most US States.

This exhorbitant price is partly due to the French

government deploying their own VAT tax *on top of* a European tax. Read: double taxation. The French tax rate is already 69% higher than the EU minimum for unleaded. Auto-related taxes are the number one source of revenues for the French government, surpassing those of individual income taxes, and taxes on corporate revenues. *La voiture* is 17% of the income of the *fisc*.

The most useful service the government spends that money on is *Bison Futé*. This 'clever buffalo' accurately predicts the amount of traffic freeways can expect before big travel weekends and holidays. Their information helps millions choose better routes, and plan the ideal time to leave.

The *least* productive government expenditure is on taxi control. The taxi police, known here as the *Boers*, crack down on Uberpool and all the other clandestine chauffeurs, writing 8 000 infractions in 2016, some rising to a fine of €15 000 and a year in prison. Regardless of protests by people against unfair competition, social dumping and tax 'optimisation,' two million people in France continue to use Uber.

Why might that be? Well, like in most big cities, official Parisian taxis don't want to accept fares to the suburbs. That's why you should always try to get in before telling the driver your destination. They're legally obligated to take you all the way to where you ask if you're already in the back seat. That didn't stop a taxi driver from telling me one Winter, "If the street gets too slippery, I'm going to leave you by the side of the road."

That was *after* being picked up from the airport. Luckily, I knew my rights and spoke French. What do other tourists do? Most licensed taxi drivers in Paris don't speak

English, don't accept credit cards, and don't use GPS. Contrast that with other world-renowned cities. All black cab drivers in London must pass a rigorous exam called 'The Knowledge' before they're licensed. Paris' exam must be called 'The Scowl.' For those who travel often from other major international destinations like Buenos Aires, Munich, and New York, it's always a shock to return and find Parisian taxis are the least accommodating.

There is a popular old French card game I played as a child, called '*Mille Bornes*' or 'A Thousand Mile Markers.' The objective is to accumulate enough cards to travel 1 000 kilometers all while the opposing players prevent you from advancing with stop signs, or flats or empty tanks. There's an expression in France which comes to mind, to put '*batons dans les roues*' or 'sticks in your wheels' to stop you from moving. That's what it's like to be a driver in France.

CHAPTER EIGHT
Borne 175 - Fall and Football

Automne et foot américain

My first Autumn in France made me homesick. So many big events back in the USA were simply non-events in France: Halloween, Thanksgiving and NFL football.

For Halloween, we went over to a friend's house in the boonies (West Yvelines) for a party and trick-or-treating. The rural village neighbor folks in Ableiges were very nice when we knocked, even though most were completely unprepared for Halloween. They brought out unwrapped marshmallows and gummy-bears, crackers, fruit and half-finished packs of biscuits. The kids didn't mind. I went as a *'gréviste'* / *'manifestant,'* a worker on strike demonstrating and shouting slogans like '*tousse ensemble, tousse ensemble*, (cough, cough)' Our friends André and Mélisande had loads of VHS tapes of the real good old Universal horror flicks from the '30s to '50s. We ended up watching The Wolfman with Lon Chaney, Jr. Modern kids and adults were completely un-scared. CGI has ruined us for the simpler frights of yore.

Thanksgiving reminded me of the time my sister-in-law, Christine, came to visit us in California at the end of November. We sent her to the butcher's to buy a turkey, but her English was so incomprehensible, they didn't understand what she wanted. She resorted to the only tools at her disposal: Franglish, onomatopoeia and pantomime.

"Please, sir, I need, *comment tu sais*, a, a big chicken!"

The butcher pointed to certain cuts, probably fowl, but she wanted him to understand a whole turkey.

"*Non, enfin, entier*, big, big chicken, BIG CHICKEN!!" She proceeded to tuck her hands in her pits, flap her elbows, and make '*kooloo, kooloo*' noises for a turkey, sounding nothing like the gobble, gobble we're taught as American children. "*Non 'cocorico,' non 'cut-cut-cut-cadette' mais 'kooloo, kooloo!!!'*"

She returned home with a large whole chicken. We laughed at her story, and wondered, "Why do languages attribute different sounds to animals?," and "Why, no matter which language you choose, the words sound nothing like what the animals say?"

"In French, it's even worse," said my wife, the language instructor. "Because each animal noise is a *different verb*. And each verb must be conjugated."

It's true, in English, we say the cow goes 'moo,' the frog goes 'ribbit,' the horse says 'neigh.' However, this construction in French inevitably deploys action verbs. And these action verbs change spelling and pronunciation, depending if it's a solo beast, or a beastess, or a troop of beasts, or if you're speaking directly to the animal, or how familiar you are with that animal, or if you're talking about what that animal did, will do, or might do sometime. All of those incidences change the form of the verb, which belongs to that species alone. For example:

Meugler (to moo): "*La vache meugle.*"
Coasser (to croak): "*Les grenouilles coassent.*"
Hennier (to whinny): "*Et vous, monsieur cheval, hennissiez-vous l'autre soir?*"

There are so many ways to get it wrong, but the French love this level of complexity in their language. For them, it's a proof of '*richesse*' and '*creativité*.' The *dictée* is still practiced weekly in grade school. Dictation used to be a national sport for adults as well, when Bernard Pivot's '*Apostrophe*' show was still on the air.

We Americans like our entertainment simple- as easy to understand as men in armor smashing into one another in the quest to displace the inflated oblong skin of a pig. The NFL playoffs were upon us, and I was in a foreign country, with no game coverage from my cable provider. The only possibility to see my beloved Rams live, was to drive into downtown Paris and sit at a bar catering to expats.

The game started at 10:30 p.m. Paris time. I arrived early at the Long Hop, a sports bar on the Left Bank, only to discover they weren't playing the game as they said they would. I had to quickly get back in my car and drive to another bar in the Saint Germain des Près district. It took me at least a half hour of circling to find a parking space. While driving, I got a call on the mobile phone from my Mom in Southern California, relaying excitedly that the Rams were in the lead at the beginning of the 2nd quarter.

Opening the door of the Frog and Princess, I was met with music videos on the screens. This bar wasn't showing NFL either. I asked as nicely as an impatient and fustrated fan could. The bar staff found a TV in the back and after several attempts the correct channel. I thanked them verbally and then REALLY thanked them by ordering several $10 mini-beers (25cl).

I was the only one really watching the game. All the young singles squished themselves around me conversing and enjoying themselves.

The game took a turn for the worse. The Rams lost momentum, then the lead, and fell too far behind to ever come back. So, I was more and more resigned to my team's fate. I started to think about what an unexpectedly winning season the Rams had had, and how happy I was to have new experiences like this one. I mean, I was in Paris where nobody cares about American football, and I was allowed to watch my team. Life's not too bad, you know?

At that moment, a French student came up to practice his English with me. He had spent some time in the 'States and was eager to talk. He introduced me to his friends, one of whom was an American guy from Philly getting ready to marry a French gal. Another was a Yank wearing a Packers hat. Both my countrymen were surprised to find the NFL on TV in a French bar on Saturday night. They were pretty out of touch with what had happened during the regular season, much less which cities still had teams.

I was kind of distracted between watching the game and talking with them. They were great folks, but the game was just too intense and I had too much personal history behind me to pull myself away. I would have liked to talk with them further. But just as I was ready to turn off my emotional juices the Rams started to drive and my new friends packed up to leave.

Down 11 points, with less than five minutes remaining, the Rams needed a touchdown, a 2-point conversion AND a field goal to tie. Not likely.

But then- it happened! Just like that! Boom-boom-boom, they got all three. The game was tied... And in the most unlikely of circumstances:

- After having a weak game, Marshall Faulk pushed over the goal line...
- The team scored a two-point conversion, which hadn't happened often that season
- Their kicker, of all players, recovered his own onside kick. I'd never seen that before.
- Then an equalising field goal as regulation ended with the two adversaries knotted up 23-23

So overtime starts, at around 2 a.m. Paris time. Last call, and we're all getting kicked out of the bar. The bouncer makes several roundups and I manage to avoid him each time. The Panthers march down the field in easy field goal range. "*S'il vous plaît, monsieur, c'est l'heure de partir.*"

I'm being escorted out of the bar, all the while looking back over my shoulder. The barman asks me if I'm crying. I wasn't, but I guess I looked really worked up. I tried to explain that the game was a do-or-die playoff and I was a little disappointed because normally it should be over in a minute and now I'll miss the end.

He said, "Oh, how about I turn the game on one of the TV's in front and you can watch through the window outside from the sidewalk?" What a nice guy!

It took him a minute to set it up. All the while, the Rams were trying to ice the Panthers' kicker with a timeout. He turned the TV toward me outside just as I saw the Panthers score to win...

But WAIT! There was a penalty, pushing the Panthers back 10 yards. Still, it didn't seem longer than a 45-yarder. Very do-able, so the Panther's kicker should make the re-try. But... he DIDN'T! Unbelievably, he missed it.

The Rams were once again alive! I was ecstatic. A crowd of one jumped and cheered on the desolate Paris street. The possessions went back'n'forth several more times with neither team scoring.

Was it destiny? How many times could the Rams resurrect themselves from the dead? It sure seemed like it was their game now. The Rams now marched down the field with ease. They were in field goal range! They could try to win it with a short kick. But this was not the style of their gambling coach, Mike Martz. The Rams kept pushing, and taking risks.

Were they oblivious to my condition? My palpitating heart? Did they give a single thought for the serenity of the Saint-Germain-des-Prés residents? Just GET IT OVER WITH! Kick the field goal and let us all get some sleep!

My wishes went unheard as they continued to pass. And pass. Until the inevitable happened... they threw an interception!

But the defense will hold, I thought. I believed. They didn't.

Now the Panthers were in field goal range. The opponent wanted to get still closer. What was it with these teams?

Then, in quick succession, a sack, a penalty and another sack pushed the Panthers back out of range. They punted back to the Rams. Back and forth again. Time ran out on the first overtime period.

The bar was long since closed. A full 20 minutes had passed with me out on the sidewalk in the early January cold. A misty rain had begun to fall. Couples strolled by, looking at this strange man with bloodshot eyes pacing and looking into the window of an empty bar. Friends regrouped to see what's next now that the bars, their homes away from home had kicked them out. Nobody caring a whit about something that had completely engrossed me for hours.

Thirty minutes had now passed since the bar had shut their doors. Would the understanding barman continue to let me watch the game for ever? He must reach his limit of tolerance soon. There was nothing left to clean inside. There was just one guy doing the books behind the bar. All his co-workers had gone home. One barmaid said goodbye to me and smiled as she left. Perhaps the agitating stranger in blue and gold had amused her, making this a night different from the others. Maybe she just wanted to see if I was any danger to her by the way I responded. She probably wondered if she'd still see me in front of that window when the sun came up the next morning.

No police came by. The street cleared out. The second overtime period was ready to begin. It had been another long wait for me, but only 10 minutes in actual time.

It was over as fast as it began. One play, a 69-yard touchdown pass by the Panthers, and all that stress and anguish was over. There was no euphoria like there would have been with a win. I just felt dead, drained and soaked through my jersey.

I drove home over empty streets with the window open, the Winter wind blowing in my face to keep me attentive.

Et les béliers blatèraient leur tristesse...

CHAPTER NINE

Borne 200 -Double Standards

Les normes doubles

Everybody knows that the administrators in the French government love their rules. Until they don't.

Restrict, control, prevent right here. *'Laissez-faire'* let it be over there.

Most areas of motorized transport in France are highly codified, regulated, certified. And then there are others without *any* oversight at all. WTF?

Scoot

If you'd like to drive a standard car, or a typical motorcycle, they make you jump through hoops. However, if you'd like to get around in a scooter, by all means, hop on and go. No questions asked. No training required. And, of course, no licensing.

It's gotta be just as natural as riding a bicycle, right? Because teens are allowed to simply revv up and merge into the same lanes as licensed motorists. Hey Sonny, want to take your scooter on the Nationale? Be our guest, as long as you maintain a minimum of 50 km/h. I've seen kids as young as 12 racing around on these things without a care. I've almost been run over on occasion. But I've never seen any of them stopped by the cops. Maybe they know there's no use bothering.

Scooters don't require a license of any kind. If, by chance, riders *are* caught in violation, police tickets can only take away points from a licensed driver. So, you can be caught for hundreds of offenses and keep on scooting. If you're under 18 in France, there's a multitude of offenses you can commit with little or no consequences. The kids are free to ride wrecklessly with impunity.

Car without a license

There's a glorified golf cart, called a *voiture sans permis*, or vehicle without a permit, also known as a Quadricycle. These putt-putts have access everywhere except freeways. Anyone can drive one of these carts if you can see over the dash. You can even putter around several passengers, at their peril. Who could possibly be harmed by an untrained pilot wheeling their way across town in a tin can about the size of a Smart car? They're not just a nuisance for real drivers, but also for pedestrians and bicyclists, because they're quiet and jump out from nowhere. But practically anyone is allowed to steer them.

Without any training whatsoever.

Camping cars

Same thing with motor homes. Large trucks require a special license. Even bigger camping cars aren't considered like these. Both are equally tricky to manoever, but only the motor home can be driven with the regular Class B license you use to drive your sedan.

Learning that this opportunity was open to me, I thought I'd try to rent one from the 'sharing economy' site Yescapa. There, I found lots of owners who only used their motor home a couple months of the year, and rented out to other citizens the rest of the time. The prices shown were half of what the professional companies would charge, and you could return on Sundays and holidays whereas the companies were closed.

I confirmed the availability of one Hymer, reserved, paid, and waited for my glorious weekend on the open road. The owner wrote that his vehicle was in the shop. Why did he confirm the reservation, then? He said he was retired, and just learning how these newfangled internet systems worked. I explained this to Yescapa customer service, and they said they'd be happy to reimburse my charges... next month.

I was a bit wary, but determined to have my long weekend, Thursday through Sunday out in the countryside. I found a Sharky for an even lower price, and reserved. Maybe this setback might save me some euro, eh? The owner texted me that she was double-booked, and asked me to cancel. I wondered how that was possible, and she said she's on a couple sites and didn't update Yescapa. I was incredulous. Yescapa was suspicious.

"Are you sure you two aren't using our site to do a deal on the side, without paying us commission?"

"Waitaminute, *you're* the guys who have now taken my money twice without providing any services. Are you sure that's even legal? Renters like Hertz don't charge until the day you pick up the car, and hotels don't charge until the day of your stay."

"OK, OK. We'll return your money now."

"*Merci*, and could you put me in contact with an owner *before* I reserve, to really make sure they're legit?" They complied, and acted as intermediary. It wasn't what they usually did, an automated service, but they had an interest to make this work, and bad customer ratings weren't going to help. The agent on the phone must've wondered if their business model relied on inventory owned by a bunch of flakes.

I asked him to check out a Knauss which was listed as available nearby. Yes, it was in good condition. Yes, it was that price. Yes, it was available, but not at the location indicated. It was currently parked in the South. He'd be happy to go fetch it for me Saturday. Didn't he see that would cut my vacation time in half? I decided to give up on the whole thing.

It's probably just as well the plan fell through. If I crossed a fellow camper, I might have been considered a gypsy.

You see, in France, one camping car driving by itself is looked at as a vacationer, or retiree behind the wheel. But two or more together is considered a band of gypsies just waiting to setup camp in your town. For a long, long time.

Spaces for recreational vehicles are strictly regulated. Nimbys force mayors to set the official lots out on the periphery, far from town centers, shopping, tourist attractions... far from everything. In the US, you can park your RV in lots of places. WalMart even welcomes drivers to park their RV in their lot overnight. The lot is empty at night anyway, and in the morning, the campers might even stock up from their store. Everybody's a winner. Then, again, US shopping centers have land to spare, whereas land is at a premium in Europe.

Some folks have found a way to stop paying that premium: just setup camp any old place they choose. It's tolerated if there are a lot of them, and they're not ethnically French. They're not called gypsies, or Roms any more, because it's more politically correct to use the term *'gens de voyage.'* Residents don't know what to do with these 'travelling folk' once they move in.

Fifty or more of their motor homes will sneak in overnight and camp in an abandoned lot, or a farmer's field, or a school playground. Then the same scene plays itself out. The citizens wail to the mayor, who asks his three municipal police officers to talk to the campers. They refuse to move, knowing there aren't enough peacekeepers to physically move them. So the standoff commences.

Residents complain, wondering what their tax funds are paying for. Surprisingly, it rarely gets out of hand. Once in a while, an angry resident will set some of their motor homes on fire. Only if there's theft, or rampant begging, or if they overstay their 'welcome' do government agencies collectively work together to build an overwhelming force of hundreds of police, tow trucks and such to clear out the camp. That's after the camping cars have been there for at least a month.

Most of the time, citizens are tolerant. Especially if the travelling folk come to the town square to play music, or dance, or sell their arts and crafts. The reasoning is, these people migrate anyway. That's what they do. If we don't make it too comfortable for them, they'll leave of their own accord. Tomorrow, they'll be in another town.

And so, one day they *do* move, without paying for their stay, without paying any fines, without contributing any taxes to the community for cleaning up and hauling away their trash.

Traffic court

France is a democratic country, governed by laws and precedents. When people wish to contest what they're accused of, there are courts and judges, and in certain cases a jury which will hear their case. Not so when it comes to traffic violations. There is no such thing as traffic court.

For someone accused of speeding, it goes like this: A letter is sent to the address of the owner on the vehicle registration, giving them three options: pay a little bit now and admit your guilt, or pay 34% more, and contest. A staggering **99%** of recipients in France pay without contesting.

If they choose to do so, the contestation must be accompanied with a letter of explanation, and sent via certified letter for €5. The other two options are when the car no longer belongs to him, or someone else was driving. The clock is ticking from the moment the owner receives the notice, and if he waits more than 45 days, the fine jumps 165% higher.

The thing is, if you pay *anything*, you're admitting

guilt. The notices don't fully explain your rights. Worse, they threaten that if you fight and lose, they can increase the fine. To whom would you protest? To the same body which gave you the ticket in the first place! The 'Center which automatically constates road infractions' in Rennes. These officials try to act as judge, jury and executioner.

The same form letter is sent to every protester: 'I have the honor to inform you that the infraction was recognized in a regular manner. Thus, it's not possible for me to favorably consider your claim. I invite you to pay the fine of...' blah blah blah. No other option is ever mentioned, even though recourse *does* exist.

Back in California, traffic court is used often, and the docket is always full. Contesting happens commonly, and defendants' rate of success is quite good. Even if they don't win, fines are often reduced by the judge. If the officer doesn't show up to argue his version of events, the accused is automatically considered innocent.

There could be many circumstances where the law wasn't broken at all, or why a law was broken justly. Once, driving in the carpool lane in Southern California with my mom, she suddenly said to pull over because she was going to be sick. There was no shoulder on the left, and on the right there were double-yellow lines. The lines were there to prevent people of vastly differing speeds to merge in and out of the carpool lane, thus avoiding accidents. It was a hefty $271 fine to cross the lines. The double lines often go on for several miles and don't open for every exit, so you'd better be sure you're comfortable being stuck in that lane for five minutes or more. The advantage is that you go a lot faster at commute times.

We were driving along at midday, so the carpool lane was clear, as were most of the other lanes to the right. After confirming that my mom really was going to lose her lunch imminently, I signalled and changed lanes, then crossed about four more lanes before reaching the shoulder and curb. Sure enough, there was a highway patrolman watching my maneuver, and he came up quickly behind us with lights flashing. I didn't even see him until we were both out of the car, because he hadn't used his siren, and I was focused on getting to my mother on the curb side.

He didn't like it one bit that we were out of the car, and instructed us to return inside immediately. I tried to explain, and my mom ignored him as she keeled over, concentrating on her insides. He wouldn't hear of it, but calmed down as he looked over my license and registration. As my mother began heaving, he ordered me to stay right there beside him, while he wrote out the ticket. Californians suspect that CHP officers have some kind of quota. If it's true, this carpool violation was worth about three speeding tickets, and our guy wasn't going to let this opportunity pass.

In traffic court, the officer admitted that my mom really did throw up, and the judge threw out the case. As the highway patrolman protested, we left the courtroom. He was one of the few policemen who showed up that day, and he was pissed that he was the only one who lost his case that morning.

The judge has a lot of power in California traffic court, and he uses that power to interpret the law, deliver swift justice and expedite fines. As you're waiting for your case to be called, you see a flurry of judgements before you. They can literally complete a dozen judgements per hour. A defendant needs to be quick on their feet, concise and convincing. It can also help to have a cute accent.

Before we met, my wife had a beat-up old car, near a run-down apartment complex in the East Bay. She had gone back to France for a month during Summer vacation. She returned to find her car windshield littered with more than a dozen parking tickets.

She went to the police station. The total bill was more than $600.

"Six hundred?!?! " She exclaimed, "but I only paid $300 for it. The car is not worth what you're asking."

"Tell it to the judge, lady."

And she did, playing up her foreign phrasing. "Excuse me, mister *Présidant*, but I did not know zat I could not park my Plimoff on Dartmoff for a monff."

"Honey," the judge corrected, "I don't know where you're from, but in America we say 'your honor,' not Mr. President." Giggles from the courtroom audience.

"Sorry mist-, er, your honour."

"Secondly, I don't know what is a 'Plimoff' or a 'Dartmoff.' Let's see. It says here you live on Dartmouth street, and your Plymouth was parked for more than a week non-stop. That section of Dartmouth has signs posted that cars parked there more than seven days will be towed. You're lucky it wasn't impounded. You were clearly informed that parking your car there for that amount of time is illegal. How do you plead?"

"Guilty sir, er, your honour."

"Oh, good," in a surprised voice. The judge continued, "So, what's the problem?"

"Well, your honour, ze fine, I cannot afford eet. Ze sex hundred, eet iz mohr zan ze car is worff."

"OK, Sweetie, tell me how much CAN you afford?"

"Pardon?"

"How much do you have?"

"In ze bank? I, um-"

"No, *on* you, at *this* very moment. How much money do you have?"

"Uh, let me check... like sex-teen."

"Would you accept a fine of sixteen dollars?"

"Oh, yes sir! ou *Prési- enfin, je veux dire* your honour."

"Perfect, pay the cashier on the way out. Next case."

The fact that France doesn't have traffic court, nor offers any body to hear complaints, is illegal as the European courts have determined. A motorist ticketed in France who wishes to contest must be given a neutral body to hear his case. However, this option is never mentioned to the accused. He's tricked into thinking there's no way out but to pay and admit guilt. So, instead of protesting through legal channels, he get's a bit tricky himself, and invents a fall guy on whom he can pass the buck. He lies, saying someone else was driving the car.

Usually this is a friend, relative or associate. Some go to extremes to pin their transgressions on someone they don't even know. A gas station attendant copied the driver's license number of Swiss sailor Alain Gautier when he stopped in for a fill-up. From then on, all of the tickets he received, as well as most of his family, were pinned on the navigator.

What's he supposed to do? He's not a lawyer, and doesn't know all the articles of the *code de la route*, and

French civil law, and European law. He probably doesn't even know how many points he has left. Drivers are not sent a letter with their remaining balance. Tickets don't note how many points the accused has remaining. Nearly a million drivers are only one ticket away from having zero points on their permit. Folks live in fear that the next ticket could take away their license.

One person who *is* a lawyer has invented an online service to help the accused easily contest certain infractions automatically. It's called EasyRad. For €54, the service will contest on your behalf, handling all the administrative junk. Unfortunately, the only promise they make is that you're practically guaranteed to not have any points taken away. The fines are almost always maintained. You rarely get called to a tribunal to hear your case. However, for someone with very few points left, whose car is absolutely necessary for their work, it's a small price to pay. Each year, more than 70 000 people lose their license in France for lack of points.

They were probably unaware for the most part before the guillotine fell. The onerous procedure license-holders need to follow to know their balance is go to the Telepoints website, fill out a form, print it, sign and send it certified (€5) with a copy of their French permit, a copy of their ID card and a SASE (also certified at €5). Only then will they send you a password. You still have to go check it yourself on the website. Deploying such a complicated process means that most people don't do it. The overwhelming majority of drivers in France don't know how many points they have remaining, nor if their license is still valid.

For this reason, and because the permit is so hard to get, an incredibly scary number of drivers on French roads have no license at all. Estimates vary from one million to 2.5 million drivers without a license, and of course, without insurance. French actress Elsa Zylberstein was convicted of driving without a license. Toulouse footballer Andy Delort was caught driving without a license. In 2007, gendarmes staging rare in-person checkpoints caught 93 000 unlicensed drivers. Imagine how many more escaped their vigilance.

Sometimes by tightening controls too much, you end up with less security.

CHAPTER TEN

Borne 225 - Christmas villages

Villages de Noël

For Christmas that first year, we drove down to my in-laws in Limousin, passing by one of my favorite French town names *Arnac-la-poste*. Read colloquially, it means 'scam the post office.'

There are many villages around France which have unintentionally racy names. In Ile-de-France alone there are *Bezons* (Let's fuck) and *Sucy-en-Brie* (Suckoff in brie).

No translation is required for the towns of *Anus* or *Condom*. For others, here's a choice list of coy town names, with their equivalents in English:

Bourré : Drunk
Trécon : Very stupid
Pisse-en-l'air : Piss in the air
Sallespisse : Filthy piss
Chilleurs-aux-bois : Shitters in the woods
Crottes-en-Pithiverais : Turds on Pithiverais
Chatte : Pussy
Montcuq : My ass
Froidcul : Cold ass
Seyssins : Her tits
Plurien : Nothing more

Many of these towns' residents don't appreciate being made fun of, nor having to replace their village signs, which keep getting stolen. Then there are others who get the joke, and invite you in on it, to laugh with them. They've created the *'Association des communes de France aux noms burlesques, pittoresques ou chantants,'* or the Association of French municipalities with burlesque, picturesque or sing-songy names. These include *Andouillé* (Numbskull), *Ballots* (Nitwits), *Beaufou* (Handsome fool), *Bellebrune* (Beautiful brown-haired girl), *Bèze* (Kiss), *Bouzillé* (Botched-up), *Cocumont* (Sucker mountain), *Corps Nuds* (Naked body), *Folles* (Crazy women), *Monteton* (My boob), *Poil* (Pubic hair), *Saint Barbant* (Saint Boring), *Simplé* (Simpleton), and *Vinsobres* (Sober wine). Residents of these towns organize an annual get-together with a market of produce from their regions, walking tours, a show and of course everyone leaves with a comical t-shirt with the host town name proudly emblazoned on it. Justement, the last meeting was held in *Marans*, which means 'Funny.'

Most highways in France are toll roads- 80% are

run by private companies. Unlike the UK, which you can criss-cross for free, the quickest way between any two major cities in France is to open your wallet. Building and managing toll roads is a high-margin, very lucrative business, with guaranteed contracts of 10-years or more. Abertis, one of the leaders in the sector made €796 Million net profit last year.

The toll roads are invariably new and in good condition. The rest stops are wholly other. Run by the same cash-rich companies that manage the toll roads, you'd figure their paid-for facilities would be better than the free gas station's, right? *Au contraire, mon frère.* If it existed, their wall display sheet of 'bathroom last cleaned' would be signed 'during the Mitterand administration.'

All toilets are open air, which means you freeze your *tuchus* on the metal bowls without seat covers in Winter. Somehow the design, without any doors and a roof much higher than the walls, manages to successfully retain the stench in the vicinity. Flushes often don't function. Perhaps weary repeat travellers never expect them to, because when the flush really is operational, they don't even try, but instead pile on. During washing-up time, you can expect neither running water, nor soap. So, naturally, there are no towels nor air machines, since there's an expectation you'll have nothing to dry.

Like many women in these dire situations, my wife has adopted the hover squat- a method without any skin-to-surface contact in such rest stops. But for this '*aire de repos*' off the *A10* on the way to Limousin, it was no use. She tippy-toed on the spaces in-between the sludge, holding her breath, until she saw the stall, the epicenter of a not very recent explosion. For a visual, think of Renton's visit to the loo in Trainspotting. It was more than she could bear.

She stormed outside to an area of foliage, tinkled and ran. She was so furious, she immediately put pen to paper in the passenger's seat. We dropped off a complaint letter at the next tollbooth, then headed down the highway without stopping the rest of the way.

From Paris, it takes about five hours to get down to Limousin, which is cow country. Seeing the hours of rural countryside go by, there's a lot of time to daydream. I harkened back to my first big road trip with a high-school friend just after graduating. We covered ground from Fayetteville, North Carolina up to Cooperstown, New York.

We were both 19, and only used to company in our own age group. Needless to say, we swore. A LOT. Sometimes we would make bets with each other how long we could go without letting a four-letter word slip out. Neither of us ever made it past one hour. Though challenged, we tried to keep it to a minimum in front of our elders.

Well, we had been on the road for about a week, talking almost exclusively to each other in sailor-ese. After a week in dumpy motels, friends of my parents were very gracious to open up their stately home in Connecticut to us over New Year's. Since I knew these people, I figured my friend would be the main source of potential embarrassment. I tried to prepare him as best I could to clean up the language before arriving.

We arrived late, and were rather tired. The host offered us some drinks, and we talked about what we'd seen so far on our whirlwind tour of the East Coast. There were a lot of funny stories, and characters, especially the gay guy running a B&B in Philly who automatically assumed that my buddy and I would share a single bed. When I described the look on our faces to our Connecticut family friend host, I let the f-word slip.

It was so natural, and I played it off looking skyward and laughing, hoping it hadn't been noticed. Not a minute later, it shot out of my mouth again, this time even louder. My friend started making faces at me, but I was on a roll and couldn't stop myself. Eventually, after several more f-bombs I tried to change the subject to something more serious, to get me out of the gutter. But I remember the host's expression being a bit pained, like someone who had just taken a bite of a detested fruitcake offered by a relative he had to be nice to. Half smiling, and unimpressed.

Now an adult in France, I pledged to make a better effort at the in-laws for Christmas. It wasn't so difficult, because it's hard to curse in French. Words an American would consider to be swearing simply roll off the tongue in mixed company here, and are easily accepted among family, even by the youngest members. I've never heard a kid being asked to watch his language, as long as he's not calling present company names directly. Body parts and private acts are described using the truck driver dictionary of words with relatives, in offices, and at the market. Street words can be heard on public télévision and radio at all hours of the day. This tends to lessen the power of the epithet. Everyday things are named or described with swear words, or prejudicial insults, which don't really have any non-dirty equivalent, such as-

'demerde-toi': or 'unshit yourself' to get out of a jam alone

'déconner': for goofing off or *'dire des conneries'* for talking garbage; the key word here is 'con' which is always versatile, but never polite, describing either an idiot or a jerk, or one acting like such a person

'crottin de chèvre': goat 'dropping' to name a small and firm round cheese

'ça me fait chier': or 'it makes me shit' to bemoan something that's bothersome

je vais *'péter les plombs'*: 'I'll fart lead' or blow my top

'péter plus haut que son cul': to get on one's high horse by 'farting higher than one's ass'

'téléphone Arabe': hearsay rapidly relayed 3rd-party or more removed

'un nègre': a ghost-writer. There's also a place on the Côte d'Azur called *'Cap Nègre'*

'une armée Méxicaine': any disorganized group of people which is much bigger than it needs to be

'cul-de-sac': or the *'ass of a bag'* describing the shape of a residential street ending; "Yes, you heard me right, Karen," who thought her high school house was better situated than mine, "you lived in a big, fat butt!"

'cul de bouteille': the bottom of a bottle

The movie version of 50 Shades of Grey, rated R in the 'States, was given the OK for French kids from 12-years-old. Honestly, they see sexier stuff at 6 p.m. on channel 2, and better written, I might add.

What they don't see is extreme violence. One of the higher-rated cop shows, Julie Lescaut, routinely featured high-speed car chases without any accidents, and suspect standoffs with nary a single shot fired. American imported police dramas with explosions and blood are shown late at night here.

Late is when we arrived in Limousin. We were offered vegetable soup, then off to bed. We'd have a lot to prepare for the big meal on Christmas day.

Food is a big deal at my in-laws. Once, I returned from an errand at 12:15 to find everyone already seated for lunch before a perfectly set table, untouched awaiting my arrival. My father-in-law admonished tersely that "*La table est sacrée!*"

At their sacred table, meals are the major topic of conversation. "What are we about to eat?" Then, *à table*, we share our opinion of what we're in the process of eating, where it came from, and compare it to other times we've had the same dish. The meal winding down, the subject turns to what we're going to eat at the next sitting.

My *belle famille* has a cellar with 1 000 wine bottles. The basement stocks hundreds of jars of green beans, chestnuts, mushrooms, and other legumes from their private garden or gathered in the nearby forest. Dozens of cans of *paté*, terrine, liver and other spreads from next-door farms line several shelves. Backyard strawberries, plums, and cherries are preserved in numerous mason jars.

Not one, not two, but *three* high-capacity freezers

line the basement wall. There is literally a *ton* of food in there. Closer to two tons. Inside, you'll find not a dozen eggs, but a dozen whole chickens, along with formerly feathered friends pheasant, quail and duck. There's rabbit, lamb and wild game like warthogs or wild boar. In another freezer, there are crustaceans and mollusks by the hundreds, along with whole poissons fished out of lakes nearby. The last freezer has *hors d'oeuvres* and desserts, mostly ice cream. Your local butcher shop or rebel cult compound has less food saved up. I know where I'm going when the end of days comes nigh.

After years of trial-and-error, I'd finally learned to pace myself for family meals in the countryside. I serve myself a little bit by little bit, and keep my wine glass full to avoid helpful relatives adding more. This method now allows me to remain upright in my chair until the end, some three-to-five hours hence.

My initial passage *à table* was a car crash, followed by a slow motion rolling descent down a never-ending ravine. Used to one-plate meals, I let them fill mine, and then accepted their offer of a second helping. A glass was downed with each. I was satisfied and distended, and feeling all warm in my mind and body. It was only the beginning. The next dish came, then another, and another. I had begun a marathon with a sprint.

Somehow my liver held out that first time, but not without severe complaint. I'd never had pain in that area before, and it was acute. A stomach ache can be alleviated with medicine to speed the transit to the end, or reject the surplus back where it came from. But the liver? It takes forever to break down and burn through all that excess. I guess the goose that gave up his force-fed *foie* had the last laugh on me.

I suffered in silence and earned the reputation from my in-laws as a good eater and drinker. Their bizarre admiration continues, though I'm much more cautious and discreet nowadays. I'm living off my forked up accomplishments of the past.

So, the Christmas meal started with the *apéritif* around noon, serving liquor and nuts. Then we sat down to oysters, a dozen each, and a dry white wine, a muscadet. My sister-in-law likes oysters with a few drops of vinegar and minced shallots. The rest of the family consumes them with a squirt of lemon, and a chaser of salted butter on bread.

The shells were carried away and replaced by an enormous platter of lobster tails, whole shrimp, and sea snails, all of which we dipped in homemade mayonnaise. Like the kids at the table, I had to wait for an experienced adult to pull off my shrimp heads, feet and tails before I could partake of the feast. Although I'm no longer shocked to see beasts presented in their raw state as 'ready for consumption,' such as fish heads, chicken heads, skin on ham (the dreaded '*couenne*'), etc. I have still not learned enough about hard-shell, flying or wiggly anatomy to get to the good bits unaided. My table guests tend to forgive my shortcomings, concluding it's not my fault I had such a poor gastronomical education. That doesn't stop sidelong looks as if I'm some alien with a runny nose who hasn't mastered the skill of using a Kleenex.

Next came a three-foot pike-*perch* fished from la Corrèze river by my nephew. Presented in all its glory with tail, skin and head intact, the fisherman quickly dissected the beast and distributed the edible parts to each plate.

Following was *foie gras* on warm toast with a syrupy white gewürztraminer. Even though it's produced under the same appellation on both sides of the Rhine, the gewürzt here is presented as Alsacian. German cuisine gets no credit here for sauerkraut, frankfurters, spätzle or flammenkueche, as they're all said to originate from Alsace, hence France.

Here, about two hours in, comes the *trou Normand* which means 'hole from Normandy.' We had our choice of pear sorbet with *eau de vie* de poire, or apple sorbet with a calvados alcohol made from Norman apples. I'm not sure if the hole is designed to be a 10-minute intermission to our gluttony, or the digging of an opening in our insides for what comes next. Either way, the 80-proof brandy and ice cream is warm going down, and you can feel it oozing into the crevasses.

Chapon, or castrated rooster was the next item on the agenda, served with a vegetable platter of beans, grilled *cêpe* mushroom bits and chestnuts. Since the *chapon* has no call to chase the hens, nor any reason to crow in the morning, the rooster becomes sedentary. He just eats and gets fat- much larger than a regular chicken, and excessively more than we needed at this advanced stage of our Christmas meal.

The rooster massacre would have been bad enough, tearing into the national symbol of France, the cock. However, we next ravaged the international symbol of toy delivery. We ate Rudolph.

Or at least we had him killed, and then thought about consuming venison. It sat there bubbling in red-nosed wine sauce as we waited for our digestive systems to catch up. Santa's lead musher died for naught that day, as the dish turned cold while the conversation continued on.

The home stretch was now in view with the placement of a salad bowl on the table. Salad thankfully is nothing more than butter lettuce, *vinaigrette* and fresh cut garlic. I grabbed a leaf and proceeded to do my duty.

Forthwith came out the cheese platter, representing at a minimum two each of cow, sheep and goat's milk varieties. Some like to mix the Roquefort blue or the Rocamadour goat with their salad, so they're brought out at the same time.

For the cheese lovers, this course can cause a singular dilemma. You know that afterward comes the dessert, so there's no use keeping red wine in your glass at the conclusion. It's best to eat bread with your cheese as well, so you'll want to have a bit of baguette handy. However, it's almost inevitable that at some point in this course, your personal table setting will run out of wine, or of bread, or of cheese. You must have all three for the completion of the tongue's holy trinity. What does one do when one has bread and cheese, but no wine? Pour a bit more wine in one's glass, of course. But is that the right amount? Now you're out of cheese, but still have a bit of bread and wine, so you re-serve yourself from the cutting board. And on and on it goes. Nirvana can't be reached until all three disappear before your eyes simultaneously.

Christmas log or '*bûche*' which is the name of the cake signals the *dénouement*. It's a breading rolled over filling, glazed with chocolate which a fork carves to look like bark, decorated with plastic trees, holiday objects, characters and sprinkled with the new fallen snow of powdered sugar. The slices show a swirl when laid flat. These were served with champagne, which is also how the drivers of the 24 hours of Le Mans celebrate completion of their feat. We had survived to the end, and now called for help, the young pulling the old up from their chairs.

On the drive back to Paris we crossed the village of *Vatan* without stopping, because it means 'get out, you!'

Arriving home we opened the response to our earlier missive about the lacking loos. The keepers of the overpriced highways defended their high standards, frequent upkeep, and praised themselves that on their toll roads, you were never more than 15 kilometers from one of these sewage heaps. No apology. No toll refund. No free coffee the next time around. *Joyeux Noël.*

CHAPTER ELEVEN
Borne 250 - Right is wrong

La droite a tort

There's a road rule in France which defies all logic. It creates the ideal conditions for an accident. You'll find it at the majority of intersections all across the land. You won't see any signs announcing that you're entering the danger zone in which the rule applies. They'd have to fill every city, town and village with hundreds of signs each. In France, it's simply accepted that you know of it, and you know the situations where its terror comes into play. Even if you come from another place where it doesn't exist. Someplace like, anywhere but France, Belgium and Switzerland. I don't know of any other countries on the entire planet which still use this law on the road.

What is this mysterious rule? It's called the '*priorité à droite*' or the 'right-hand right of way.' How does it work? Say you're driving on the main road, through the village center or city downtown. There are no tri-color lights in this section, no road signs to guide you, but you're not worried. After all, you're on the main drag, zipping past smaller side streets. These are not broad avenues on your right, mind you. They're tiny one-lane neighborhood streets, or narrower, shorter city streets and driveways. They couldn't possibly present any danger, could they?

Well, you *should* be worried. *Very* worried. Because cars poking out from these little side streets have the right of way in France.

Imagine the equivalent in America. Every side street, and every house with a driveway touching the main road could just merge without warning into the street, or turn left in front of moving traffic with impertinence. No looking left and right before engaging. No flicking the turn signal. Just pull out, and the rest of the world be damned.

If their sudden maneuver causes the Ford on the left to t-bone their Toyota, it's the Ford's fault, not theirs. If they merge unscathed, but the guy occupying the lane has to slam on his brakes, and the lady behind him plows into his rear bumper, it's her fault, not his. The piddling side-streeter is never at fault, because the right-hand right of way is on their side.

This means that at most intersections you cross, the biggest danger isn't straight ahead, it's on your right, ready to pounce, and invisible to you until it's too late. How are you supposed to accommodate for this anomaly? Simple, instead of watching where you're going, you must look around each and every corner to the right, at every single side street.

Well, since there are no signs posted, when do you know that the right-hand right-of-way is in effect? Quite simple, really. It's in the center of town... and also *near* the center... well, pretty much the whole town... except that part on the outskirts which is just fields, but quite close to where the town begins, or ends... or in-between two parts of the same town which has a couple separate principal areas.

So, when in doubt, slam on your brakes.

There are exceptions, of course. If the street to the right ends with a Stop sign, or a solid white line, the side street driver must halt and give way to the traffic on the main road. Stop signs are extremely rare. There's only one stop sign in all of Paris. So, as a main road driver, not only do you need to watch for signs and lines in your *own lane*, you need to pay attention to the signs and lines on the *side streets*. They're not there for you, but they concern you. How you read the back of a sign is beyond my comprehension.

A dashed, or dotted line on the asphalt doesn't help. They don't need to stop at a dashed line, but they should yield to traffic on the main road. If it's a zebra crossing, the side-street speeder only slightly slows down before cutting you off. From the main road, the dotted line and crosswalk on a side street look identical until you're about level with them. That is, if they've been painted recently. Some are so worn by traffic, you don't know which car should yield.

What if you're on a pretty long, rather big street, and you come up to another street around the same size and shape? Which of you is on the main road, and which is on the side street? What about cities and towns with several main arteries? Well, luckily, the more complex and dense and populated an area becomes, the more likely they are to have invested in tricolor lights, or signs to guide drivers. You know, a normal infrastructure, instead of some invisible arbitrary and dangerous relic law, written in 1910 before lights and signs.

Some nostalgic nincompoops would gladly go back to that olde-tyme layout. They love the right-hand right-of-way so much they want to do away with all signal lights altogether. The theory is that without any indications at all, drivers would slow down coming to an intersection and let the drivers on the right go first, thus avoiding accidents and making the traffic flow. The problem is people don't do that in real life. Especially not in Latin cultures.

Have you ever seen what happens when the *Métro* train arrives in Paris? A crowd squeezes in front of the doors as the train stops. The doors open and the platform people push in without a care for the poor souls trying to exit. That's the chaos expected at *carrefours* across this country if the stoplights disappear.

Test-time!

So, for my math-loving fonctionnaires, here's a little word problem *contrôle* (quiz) for you:

You're driving the speed-limit of 50 km/h happily through a town, and so is every other car. It's the speed restriction, after all, when inside the city limits everywhere in France. That means all cars are moving at 13 meters per second. At this speed, the driver's handbook advises that you need 30 meters of stopping distance. That's 15 meters reaction time in half a second, and 15 meters more to come to a complete halt.

All good so far on the numbers? OK, let's continue.

You breeze to a normal town intersection, a square which is six meters wide and six meters long. It is without a stop sign, nor a yield, nor a light, nor a crosswalk- in other words, just like most intersections. However, like most town centers, all parking spaces are filled, right up to the corner. The buildings practically come to the corner as well. The buildings are separated from the street by a small strip called a *trottoir*, which is just wide enough for a *chaussure* to mix with a *crotte de chien*.

Now, due to the cars and buildings blocking your view, the angle is such that your front bumper is only four meters from the front line of the intersection square at the time when someone sitting in the driver's seat COULD possibly see a car coming from the right, a car that's also four meters from that same intersection. The car on the right chugs along at 50km/h like you, as mentioned before. In only one second he's fully in your lane. He doesn't look left. Why should he? He's secure that the law is on his side, and he can make a right turn completely oblivious to the world outside his windshield. Meanwhile, you're obliged to slam on your brakes.

So, here's your quiz Question: "Is there any way to avoid a collision?"

answer: yes- change the stupid law!!!

CHAPTER TWELVE

Borne 275 - New Year

Bon Année

Every New Year's eve here, a bizarre tradition perpetuates. Thousands of cars are burned across France. At least 5 000 cars are set ablaze on each of Saint Sylvester and Bastille Day. In the riots of 2005, more than 8 000 cars were burned throughout the country. More than 50 000 cars are burned annually in France.

There are nicer traditions, however. There's one in France at the beginning of January which alludes to the Epiphany. They make a '*Galette des Rois*' or King's Cake. Inside they put a little ceramic doodad that's about as big as the end of your pinky. The kids know it's in there but they don't know where. So slices are distributed and all the kids eat very carefully, hoping their next bite will contain the prize. If it does, they get to be King, or Queen for the day and get to wear the crown that goes with the cake.

For the first time in my life, I lived in an area with four seasons. Northern California has three distinct seasons, but it never snows in the Bay Area. SoCal is even blander, with barely any rain, and two seasons. The hills are scorched brown from April to October. Christmas and New Year in LA are depressing.

In Le Vésinet, we had snow right outside our front door. The parks and open spaces called the kid in me outside to play. Experiencing such changing weather made me more impulsive. In California, we could play basketball today or tomorrow. No rush. The court would always be there, dry and ready. In France, I never knew how long a good thing would last. So I seized the moment at every occasion.

Five days after it snowed, it shot up to 12 degrees celsius (54° farenheit) and it was very nice. But very windy. I decided to take Paul out to fly a kite that my California friend Nancy got for us. Paul got on one of those pedal-less European trainers, and we biked over to a long green 'allée' leading from the residential area right up to the train station. We tried to find a launch area away from the tall trees on either side of the wide lawn.

It was pretty easy to get the kite up, but hard to keep it up. Paul loved pulling the string and running into the wind. He didn't like paying attention where the kite actually flew. A couple times it got caught slightly on some low branches. A little tug got it loose each time.

We got tired of running with the kite, and decided to let it fly higher, hoping that the wind was stronger up there. It was. Much stronger. And the fierce wind made the kite whip all around and do cool tricks without any effort.

Paul saw this and got very excited, tugging at my arm to let him try. I was barely holding on myself, but I relented to his wishes. Grabbing hold, he started running with the wind, giggling madly, arms outstretched to the sky. As he was running in the direction of the street which traversed the park, I shouted for him to stop. Just before he reached the curb, he halted, and let go. The kite shot off like a rocket in the direction of the train station and planted itself high in the last tree before the rails.

I ran after the spool, which had unspun to its last turn of string. The string was slowed by a power cord about 20 feet over my head. I grabbed ahold and ran back to the other side where Paul was waiting. All the time I was furiously winding up the loose thread. I had to run back quite a ways, before where I began, until all the slack was out. I wound and wound and wound moving forward just inches at a time. What did they give me, like a mile of string or what? Several hefty tugs after about five minutes released the kite from one tree and soon brought it into a middle branch three trees closer. There it stayed. Stuck.

The string first snapped at the power line. Then approaching the tree and pulling, the other part of the string also broke. Looking up, I was explaining to Paul that this was the end of our adventure.

When out of the gate of a nearby house came a father and his two sons, all eager to help. He spoke with an accent. The soccer ball they offered didn't work, so the man said he'd go get a branch. The branch he brought back wasn't long enough, so he went back again to get a ladder. He climbed up holding the forked branch, which touched the kite, but couldn't get a hold of it. We were all laughing, and as he spoke more, I guessed he was Italian. I suggested turning the branch like trying to grab a length of spaghetti. Sure enough, he trapped the trailing tail and with a yank, our kite was free.

I thought that was nice enough, rescuing our toy, but then he invited us in for a drink! I had a beer and Paul an orange juice as we got to know each other. His wife was German and the kids were 6 and 7 and each trilingual. One used to have Paul's teacher, and still goes to the same school. They'd only lived in Le Vésinet for two years, leaving Paris when it got too cramped with the kids. We shared some common feelings about how welcoming a community it is, and a similar appreciation for the greenery and parks, in a place so close to the big city.

I left thinking that the world really is small, strangers do have much in common, and it takes so little to establish a connection.

CHAPTER THIRTEEN

Borne 300 - Bike follies II

Vélo en folie II

Bicycling in Paris wasn't as developed back in 2004. Bikes were individually owned, and lugged precariously through turnstiles, or illegally boarded on trams. There still aren't any front-of-bus carriers like in the Bay Area. Vélib bikes appeared within the city limits only in 2007.

In the Spring of 2004, I learned about the regular ritual of bike riding through Paris. I heard there was going to be another ride organized at 10 p.m. on Friday, leaving from the front of the *Hôtel de Ville* (City Hall). It was such unexpectedly good weather that April, I decided to join at the very last minute.

I put Paul to bed at 9 p.m. I was dressed and riding to the Le Vésinet station at 9:15. At 9:34 I hopped on the RER A. I arrived at Châtelet-Les Halles station at 9:58 p.m.! Two minutes to spare. I still had to run up stairs and through tunnels to find the exit to the Rue de Rivoli. Let me tell you, it's not easy to get a mountain bike and my caboose through those Métro turnstiles! My head popped above ground, and I asked somebody to direct me. I raced my bike several blocks down the street, hoping the group would take off late, or at least in my direction. I had no reason to worry. The group was large and loud and easy to find. I fell right in and we were off.

I heard someone say that we were 650 strong in total. It was just like being in the middle of a Critical Mass bike rally in San Francisco. The organizers were great. They were all excellent riders, in bright orange, leading the way in front of us, creating a kind of extended human wall on the right and left, and protecting our flanks. So we could ride with ease right down the middle of the wide Parisian boulevards, and at a relaxed pace so we could take in the view. One guy had hooked up a sound system with loud electronic dance music blasting from his handlebars. It created quite an atmosphere. We rode past so many of the major monuments and sites. There's a magic feeling bumping over cobblestone streets.

A young couple rode up to me. The girl was a little rowdy, singing an '80s French pop song. We started talking and they heard my accent. "I looooove American!" she said, and egged me on to sing songs in English. We rode for the next hour, exchanging lyrics. Most of the time, we weren't able to finish more than a chorus together. I was asked to translate stuff like "that deaf, dumb and blind boy, sho' plays a mean pinball!" I was happy to contribute a little bit of culture to the conversation.

At 12:30 a.m., just a few blocks from making a complete circle, the cobblestones started to feel really hard, and then I began to wobble. I stopped completely. I had a flat. Again!? So flat in fact, that the tire was off the rim, and blocking the brakes. My pump wasn't sufficient to bring the tire to rolling pressure. I called out to the boyfriend, who stopped and circled back. But he didn't have any tools. I said I'd just push the bike (holding up the back tire) to the rendez-vous point, where the emergency team should be able to help me out.

He said "didn't you mention that you were heading home by public transport?" I said it'd be no problem because the trains run until 2 a.m. He said he's not so sure, because he takes the Métro and the last, last train is at 1 a.m. He advised me to hoof it to the nearest station. I took his advice. If you think it's hard racing through the Métro and turnstiles with a mountain bike, try it carrying a mountain bike with a back tire that won't roll!

I made it down to the platform five minutes before the last, last train heading back West out of the city. While waiting, I was serenaded by a group of Spanish students, who had had too much to drink, but weren't through with their fun. There were many tunes I didn't recognize, but I did pick out "La Bamba" and "Volaré". Don't ask me why they were singing an Italian standard.

It was a great evening, made even better because, for the first time EVER, Paul let Aurore and I sleep in until 10 a.m. on a Saturday! When we awoke, he was playing quietly by himself in his room.

CHAPTER FOURTEEN

Borne 325 - Commuter train

Train aux heures de pointe

I'm in a middle car on the commuter train and we're stopped on the track. Five minutes go by. Tick-tick. 10 minutes. Tock-tock.

The conductor finally gets on the loudspeaker and says, "I know this is a shitty situation, but it's no use banging on my door!"

More minutes pass. He blames 'signal problems' for our delay and has no further info. Out the window, I notice a group of five rail workers in orange vests on another track smoking and chatting casually. Another train full of commuters comes and blocks my view as it crawls forward, and then stops in turn.

The sun is halfway to its peak, and it shines over the other train's roof, through my window, and heats up my face. I've got a 20-minute tan on my left cheek now. I'm looking around for an open seat facing the other way, to get my right side.

Then, without any announcement, the train lurches forward, and lopes maybe 50 meters more before stopping anew. This gives me a view of three more orange vests on the right side, one sitting on the stoop, on his smoke break, at 9:48 a.m. Apparently not appreciating being gawked at by 500 people late for their jobs, he gets up in the direction to join his comrades on a leisurely stroll to the station, which is about a five-minute walk away.

I get up and stretch my legs, take off my sweater and jacket, because I'm quite warm now. I find a seat on the right side, but I must lean forward to continue my tanning and typing. People phone. People text. They sigh.

Existential thoughts enter my head. What if we never leave? Is this my destiny? What is the meaning of work? Are these my new companions for life? I don't think so, because in all this time nobody has said a single word to anyone else in this car. Some other trains around us on the other dozen tracks have moved on, but not ours. Is there no free will? Are we all lemmings? How long until someone makes a break for it? How long until someone pees on the floor?

My head shakes involuntarily. My eyes blink. I decide to wipe those thoughts from my mind. I take my work laptop and dive into a spreadsheet. Another hopeful announcement from the conductor and the car comes alive with voices. First in exclamations to no one in particular, then, in actual exchanges with strangers they've just passed an hour with in brightly lit silence.

That's faith. There's belief we'll soon be moving. The plans we made before boarding can still be accomplished. Phones ring, indicating we're missed, we're needed. The world outside remembers us.

The motor hums louder. It idles. The air comes on. Oh, that's why. Of, course. After the last week of rain, it's become a beautiful Spring day. Somewhere people are strolling along the riverside. Birds are chirping, and guiding their young out of the nest to explore, to discover to fly.

Several minutes hence, the car remains still and the mood turns sour. People tap. People snap gum. People tsk tsk.

We start to move. We keep moving. This train might actually go somewhere. We stop at the quay. Everybody gets up and moves toward the door. There's relief as we disembark.

But something's amiss. I don't recognize where I am. Is this a weigh station in purgatory. No it's the Pont Cardinet, a disused station, the last one before our destination. There's been no announcement. Is this our final stop? Where do I go from here? Pont Cardinet doesn't connect where I need to go. It's far from everything, and has no connections to speak of. No Métro, no tram no bus. This isn't helping anyone. A wave of people flows back to the cars. Do they know something I don't?

I get back on my former train while I look to see if I have a map of Paris. Might as well be on board if they make an announcement. They do, saying we're moving on. The buzz sounds, the doors close abruptly and many of our former car-dwellers, people we've spent an hour with, are stranded on the quay. We weren't really that close. The rest of us, we go. And go.

In a couple minutes, the familiar grey and black iron works of Saint Lazare appears. We've arrived, 80 minutes late, triple my normal commute time. For leg one.

There will be a continuation. Part two of the commute: the Métro. 13 more stops and I could be there. Concievably. I decide to board the train. I haven't lost my faith.

CHAPTER FIFTEEN

Borne 350 - Radar

Les Radars

In *2004*, France began the widespread deployment of speed cameras, the dreaded *'radar automatique.'* These machines, permanently fixed in concrete, sprung up everywhere. Overnight, *gendarmes* disappeared, giving way to the unfeeling eyes of 4 150 radar robots.

Between 2003 and 2006, the number of infractions captured on French roads jumped 100%. This huge jump had nothing to do with drivers breaking the law more often. Simply, the ever-watchful eye of the radars let nothing pass unpunished. From 2006 to 2012, infractions leaped another 75% higher. Today, more than 20 million radar photos are taken each year. Speeding is the number one infraction captured, representing 58% of tickets.

For as little as 5 km/h (3 mph) over the limit, the radar snaps a picture, and an automated machine sends a pic to the car owner with the bill. The vast majority of tickets are for speeds less than 10 km/h (6 mph) over the limit. France is the only country in Europe which takes away points for infractions under 10km/h over the speed limit. A whopping 25% of tickets are for 1 or 2 km/h over.

Using the provided TIP direct debit form instead of a check to pay the fine automates the processing. Machines do practically all the notification and collection. Only 7% of infractions are actually witnessed and recorded by a human.

The machines are not infallible. A radar camera clocked a parked bus at 74 km/h. Another artisan in a kangoo received a notification for travelling at a physically impossible 600 km/h. But even when the machines screw up, the State *still* wins. In 2009, nearly 10 000 ticket notifications were simply lost, and never sent. Were the accused let off the hook? Hardly. Two months later each person finally *did* receive a notification, informing them that because they hadn't paid by the first deadline, their fine was now four times higher! They each had to pay €375 and were offered no recourse.

Another radar, on the A86 at Drancy, was re-calibrated down to 70 km/h during road works. However, the authorities neglected to inform motorists with signs indicating the new speed limit. The result was that hundreds, if not thousands driving under the posted 80 km/h received tickets. The authority in the matter refused to exonerate any of the infractions.

If you think the authorities are using radars to tell the populace to go and fuck themselves, you're right! Literally. In Eaucourt-sur-Somme, a pedagogical radar without a camera was set up to educate drivers with a warning message when they sped. Drivers going above 50 km/h were shown the words 'FUCK YOU' in bright red letters. The radar insulted drivers for a week.

A government report, cited in Auto Plus magazine in 2008, stated that in order to properly read the speed of passing cars, the radar had to be installed at precisely a 25-degree angle to the road. The report said that many of the radars were angled improperly, attributing higher speeds than those to which the automobiles were actually travelling. No bother, those who protested were considered guilty. To prove their innocence would have required that an *'huissier de justice,'* a government-mandated process server, provide conclusive evidence showing that the measurements used by the machine were off. No *huissier* in their right mind would take the job.

The government's announced objective of radar profligacy has been to reduce accidents. Has it worked? Well, after an initial dip downward in the first couple years, during the subsequent decade the number of road deaths remained essentially stable. Maybe drivers aren't the problem. At least a third of those killed on the road are pedestrians. Jay-walking is a routine practice exercised in the French culture. In a CNRS study, 42% of Pedestrians in Strasbourg crossed against a don't walk sign. This compared to only 2% in Nogoya, Japan. This French behavior contributed to 10 000 pedestrian injuries last year, and 540 deaths, a 14% increase.

Only in 2017 have the authorities tried to raise awareness of the dangers of jay-walking, with an ad campaign where they scared the hell out of people in the act. When in the middle of a perfectly unthreatened crosswalk, loudspeakers rang out screeching brakes, to the panic of the pedestrians. Their instant reactions were captured with a photo, which was immediately posted to an ad kiosk. The people saw their alarmed expressions when they arrived on the other side out of breath.

Maybe future ad campaigns might be able to do what the radars haven't: make the roads safer. For each of the past three years overall road deaths in France have actually gone UP, and they're headed for their 4th consecutive year of greater fatalities. Read: NO improvement. What HAS increased is the bank account of the *Trésor Public*. More than half of their take from fines hasn't been spent on anything to do with road security.

The government's 'safety' discourse isn't convincing. An Inserm research report showed 93% of drivers don't want any more radars. The populace is fed-up with entrapment by machines.

This trick of taxation without police presentation operates 24/7/365, and it's very, very profitable. In 2015, €789 million was pocketed through radars. The record in one three-hour period is more than 1 200 tickets- by one radar camera. The all-time champion is the radar in Clarafond, on the A40 toward Lyon, which consistently picks off 377 motorists a day, 137 700 per year. At an average of €75 per ticket, that's more than €10 million to the State, *each* year, from *ONE* camera. Puts Snapchat's business model to shame.

On one 18 kilometer stretch of the Dupleix A86,

between Rueil-Malmaison and Vélizy, no fewer than 12 radar cameras have been installed. What's more, drivers actually PAY for the privilege of perusal by the police paparazzi. That's right, it's a toll road which costs €9.30 one-way. In 2013, the radars of this segment flashed 92 000 times.

With the advent of radar cameras, here was a foolproof system with no escape for scofflaws, right?

Well, once they're setup, the radar camera's coordinates are known, and can be shared. It's perfectly legal for anyone to tell you where the radars are. A court decision found a Facebook group site was within their rights to tally and post the position of every radar in France. Another citizen blog regularly publishes the planning of mobile radar speed traps setup temporarily in certain municipalities. However, if you're caught *in the car* using a radar detector, it's a fine of €1 500 and removal of six points. This is the most points you can have taken away at one time without losing your license. This is as severe as the penalty for drunk driving. You don't mess with *Pierre's portefeuille.*

Drivers can try to get advanced warning by using tools like Coyote, a paid service used by five million Europeans, or Waze, a free app used by 20 million drivers in France. The iCoyote was a Top 10 app in terms of revenue generated by French users last year. France is the only country where Coyote came in the top 10, showing the extreme necessity to detect and combat radars here. They're not called 'radar detectors,' which are illegal. To get around that designation, these applications indicate 'danger zones' which have been noted by the app developer, or by users connected to the platform. In France, 17% of users actively notify Waze or other apps in real time when they see police or mobile radar speed traps.

Unfortunately, the apps are quite unbearable to listen to. They have to hide the real location of the radars among other 'dangers.' The apps are forced by the authorities to make the zone several kilometers long rather than pinpointing the radars. Did I mention there are *four thousand* radars? The result is that the damn thing just beeps all the time. Many taxis use them, so a ride to the airport is a litany of annoying robot noises.

French drivers who DO get caught have some way of shirking point removal: ask for the photo. With 90% of radars, the picture is taken from the back, so no way to tell who's driving. If the photo shows two cars, the accused could say that the *other* car set off the radar detector. The ones from the front could be blurry, or dark at night. In this case, the accused doesn't need to say who WAS the driver, only that he WASN'T. He'll likely be asked to pay the fine anyway, but won't lose any points.

What's even more clever is to register the car in the name of someone who can't have points taken away. A car from Caen committed 70 traffic violations in three years without losing a single point for the drivers. How? The *carte grise* was assigned to their 4-year-old. This is perfectly legal.

Sneaky foreigners

20% of infractions in France are made by cars with foreign plates. More than 500 000 British drivers get flashed annually by radars in France, and avoid any penalty. This is because the different European countries don't share license and registration information with each other.

A Mercedes with Romanian plates was flashed speeding in Belgium 136 times in only nine months. Another Mercedes with license plates from Great Britain was caught on Florentine cameras speeding a whopping 1 500 times in only a couple weeks.

Similar percentages of foreign freeloaders are seen in other European countries, like Germany.

On a business trip near Stuttgart, where Mercedes are built, I set my personal record of 200km/h in a rented VW Polo on the Autobahn. I smiled to myself- and was promptly blown past by a BMW that didn't break a sweat. In Germany, they don't consider speed to be the main cause of accidents. Neither the UK, where the Government has admitted exceeding the speed limit is a contributory factor in only 6% of accidents. The number one cause, in 60% of cases, is that the road is poorly designed. When there's an accident on the Autobahn, they send out surveyors. Is the turn angle too severe? Does the grade reduce reaction time to unacceptable levels? Are the sightlines creating blind spots? A report is completed, and changes are made to the design, or by enacting a speed limit on that section of freeway.

When it's not the road, the main culprit is distance, or drivers not leaving enough of it between themselves and the car in front of them. Following too closely is a serious offense in Germany, and a hefty fine. I've never been tailgated in Germany. And it works. The fatality rate on the Autobahn is a measly 1.9 deaths per *billion* kilometres travelled. It's no wonder the fatality rate is higher in France- 76% of French drivers admit they don't respect the posted security distances.

German drivers can carry this healthy behavior onto French roads, going over the limit if they choose, knowing a radar photo will never penalise them. Each country has different license plates, and European governments don't share driver infractions with each other. Even if they did, you don't see one country enforcing a road penalty that took place in another country.

That doesn't stop the French government from trying. The radar revenues headquarters in Rennes, Antai, has a comprehensive website in English, German, Italian, Dutch and Spanish. This, from a country which hardly translates *any* of its government websites. The CPAM (national healthcare), Préfecture (DMV) and Service Public (directory of government services) are all French-only. When they have cash to collect, it's "How may I help you?" When they already have your money, and you're needing services that your tax funds have paid for, it's "*Je n'ai rien compris, pouvez-vous répéter votre demande, en français?*"

Some of the tickets of local license plates can present difficulties in collection of fines: rental cars. Florence, Italy, issues more than €50 million in traffic tickets each year, a good percentage of them for rental cars with Italian plates.

European countries will sure try their level best to collect remotely by sending notices across borders. Düsseldorf meter maids sent a parking ticket and letter to the address on my California driver's license. It explained in perfectly clear German how it would be better to pay now before the penalties kicked in. I don't think they've ever collected.

The Swiss radar system went the extra mile to write to me in English, accompanied by a blurry image of a speeder looking smart in dark glasses behind the wheel of a rental near Lake Leman. The rental car company tried to collude with the government by deducting the amount from my credit card. I refused the charges, stating factually that I was being billed for a service which I did not order, nor did the debitor have my consent. The money was promptly restored. Credit cards are neat.

My Swiss friends wrote twice more, but were not any more successful attempting to collect directly. I saw the holes in their cheesy plan. True to their nature, Swiss agents felt that an outlaw would be compelled to pay up when presented with photographic evidence. *Nein.*

Cultures vary widely on compliance to rules, from extremes on the North and South of the global *Mason-Dixon* line. United Nations workers with diplomatic plates have famously *shirked* the system, owing millions in outstanding parking fines to the city of New York. The worst offenders invariably come from the Middle East and Africa. Kuwait tops the list, with 246 violations- *per diplomat.* Here, at last, was something the Kuwaitis and I could agree upon. Swedish and British diplomats paid every single ticket. Suckers!

Even my fellow Americans can get fed-up with being governed by Gort. The local politicians of Montgomery, Alabama bought into a sales pitch by American Traffic Solutions showing how 'Bama could make big bucks by outsourcing tickets and throwing due process into the circular file. Montgomery even committed to a volume of revenues before the first robo-infraction was recorded. Then, they caught a lawyer in their web: Adam

MacLeod.

Mr. MacLeod fought the ticket, and after some trouble, was given a hearing. At trial, he established that the identity of the driver was unknown, the car owner was not seen at the scene, and the police officer who signed the affidavit did not witness the infraction. In fact, there were no witnesses put forth at all by the prosecution. The judge dismissed the ticket, but as of this writing the accused has still not recovered the money he was fined. Because of this, and other protests, the attorney general of Alabama repealed all traffic camera laws in the state.

After starting out like France, planting radars a-go-go in the United Kingdom, Britain has now rolled back. The UK eliminated 60% of their radar cameras since 2009, and still remained in the top four safest countries to drive in Europe. Denmark, which doesn't have a *single* radar camera, has half as many fatal accidents per capita as France.

Radar money is like a drug. Instead of going cold turkey, the French government would need to find another fix of revenue elsewhere to replace their radar high. Like a true addict, they aren't even looking to cut back. To make up for their shortfall in attaining their unreachable goal of less than 2000 road fatalities by 2020, gendarmes are again performing stings on the streets. Dozens of them descend on one area, with a goal of writing a thousand tickets in an afternoon.

Nearly two dozen gendarmes descended on one section of the Vallée de Chevreuse for an entire afternoon. After pulling over 310 motorcycles, they were only able to find 41 infractions. This shows a large majority of the populace respecting the law, and the inefficacy of police state bullying.

CHAPTER SIXTEEN
Borne 375 - Lifer

A vie

A California driver's license is good for five years (four up until recently). Renewal is painless the first time, it can be done online and they mail you the new one. I had done this from France, but by the April 2005 expiration date, my license still hadn't arrived at my California address.

Tina, the nice lady who I reached on the phone at the DMV in Sacramento, said since the original mailing of my license (back in mid-March) had slipped into the ether, she'd send me out a new one, which should arrive sometime within the next three weeks.

I asked my Cali crew to be on the lookout for a two

by three-inch card with a picture of a movie-star on the front. Tina was good for her word, and by May, I had four more years, four more years...

Today, after two cycles of five years, or ten years of automatic California driver's license renewals, you've got to physically go down to the DMV so they have a look at you, test your eyesight, get an updated photo and generally make sure you're not dead or dying. This re-checking happens for all license-holders until one day it gets taken away, hopefully *before* the aging person becomes a danger behind the wheel.

In the UK, your license expires when you become 70 years old, unless you prove that you're otherwise road-worthy. There's even a television program on ITV called the '100 year old driving school.'

In France, once you complete the process for the first time, the French license is good for **LIFE**. That's right, no renewal paperwork, no more visits to the *Préfecture*- EVER! No highway patrolman will come to your door. If you become blind, senile or lose a leg, just keep truckin' on down the *Autoroute*. If you use nothing but the *Métro* for two decades, a very common occurrence, don't worry, you can pop back in a jalopy any time. It's just like riding a bicycle – you never forget, and the laws never change, of course.

If you ever want a surefire laugh, ask to see an older French person's pink passport-sized permit. Compare the wide-eyed 18-year-old in the black-and-white photo to the bluehair in front of you. Do you see any resemblance at all? Do you think a policeman could tell if it was the same person?

Yet, that's the official document, which folks here carry around with them for their entire lives. A lifetime- just think about that for a moment. Several French citizens have lived to be 120 years old. Since life expectancy in France is among the highest in the world, for the average person, that pink paper permit will remain valid for 70 years!

I've never run across a French person who questioned the forever nature of their permit. The feeling is they've earned it. It's an acquired right. They'll never, ever give it up, and wouldn't go through the process again because it's so painful!

Here is a sample of ordeals which are typically easier, less expensive and take less time than getting a French driver's license:

- Permit to pilot a 40-foot sailboat in French waters (you're ready now, no certification of any kind required)
- Obtaining a building permit for a home extension drawn up by an architect
- Becoming a US state certified or licensed esthetician (also easier in some states to become a plumber, electrician, etc.)
- Naturalizing as a French citizen

A game show on France 2 this past May called '*Tout le monde joue avec la code de la route*' or 'Everybody plays with the driving code' asked contestants on the set, in the audience and at home to try and re-pass the theoretical portion. Both hosts, and the vast majority of those who played failed.

The process is so damn hard, many try and cheat the tests, and even *pay* for the priviledge. French singer Kendji Girac paid €1 500 to have a criminal buzz him the correct answers while he was taking the theoretical portion. The criminals pocketed at least €740 000 from hundreds of people who were fed up from flunking the incredibly difficult test. It's faster and cheaper than failing the test multiple times, which is a situation much more common than passing the first time. Even if they got away with it, the candidates would still need to go through the half-hour driving portion, with its own set of challenges, and pass *that* with flying colors. There's no way to fake yourself through the variables of changing road conditions, traffic and itinerary with an inflexible examiner.

Passing the driving test is easier in the USA, it's true. No matter which State in which you choose to get your license, it'll take less time, you'll have fewer questions, which will be simpler, and the behind-the-wheel portion will be more straightforward and shorter than in France.

In California, you pay only $33 to take a test of 46 questions, all with one simple answer among four choices. Only 38 right (83%, a B-) are needed to pass the written portion. California even offers the written test in 31 languages. France offers their theoretical/written test in *one* language. Even the Chinese have a separate driving test in English for foreigners.

In California, if you fail in the morning, you can try again that same afternoon. This has hardly changed since I took the test in 1985.

Of course, there are traps. One I remember from my test went something like this:
Bicycles…:
A_____ are hard to see
B_____ always have the right of way
C_____ cannot ride on city streets
D_____ shouldn't pass cars

The correct answer was A. With a good deal of common sense, and not a lot of road-specific knowledge, you could get many of the questions right in the USA.

Once you pass and obtain a learner's permit, you can immediately drive with *any* other adult license holder for six months before you have to try the behind-the-wheel test with an examiner. The behind-the-wheel test is shorter than in Europe, the grading isn't as severe, and almost all students use an automatic vehicle that they're familiar with, like their parents' car.

Succeeding this abbreviated process doesn't mean that new American license holders are less prepared. They're ready to go for the road conditions they're likely to encounter in their US state.

California is a place with five different climates, including deserts and the Rocky Mountains. California drivers deal with challenges unknown elsewhere, like legal right-turns on a red light, curbing your wheels to park on San Francisco hills. Prospective California drivers are tested on these things.

Between the US and Europe, there's also a difference in philosophy. Driving in the US is considered a right. Depriving a citizen of their license is akin to taking away their freedom, and in most cases, their livelihood.

In Europe, the car is considered as a potential weapon, and the driver as a potential criminal. Weapons are highly regulated here. In France, to obtain a single-cartridge shotgun one must submit to a background check. You must pass tests before the authorities demonstrating proper use, before being granted a permit and the right to own. A gun owner must then store his unloaded firearm under lock and key. At any moment, an inspector may show up at their door to verify that the gun is properly and safely stored. If not, the weapon is confiscated, the owner's permit revoked and a fine is issued.

CHAPTER SEVENTEEN

Borne 400 - Driver's Ed - signup

Auto-école- inscription

Despite the many obstacles I faced as a foreigner, it appeared that I was just pig-headed enough to stick around in France. My legal standing as a driver was precarious. The law said you had to get a French license within a year of arriving in France. Sure, I might be able to skate by on a technicality. After all, I *was* out of the country at least once a month on business trips. I had the passport stamps to prove it. Well, on the UK trips anyway. The rest of the European Union was now open borders without any checks or patrols. Took away all my potential passport souvenir stamps. And my excuses. Damn Schengen!

Even without the passport, if stopped, I could produce a horrendous accent in French that really didn't require much effort at all. 'This guy must be a newcomer,' the cop would say. If they caught me with the fact that I'd been renting a home longer than a year, or had a bank account here for more than a year, etc., I'd just say, "sure, but I haven't been *DRIVING* that whole time." It's true, I relied almost exclusively on public transportation.

I needn't have bothered with all the cloak-and-dagger, and memorizing invented stories. I was never pulled over. The cops I didn't need to worry about. Like the demise of Al Capone, it was the pencil-pushers that would get me.

"What if you get in an accident?" friends would ask.

"Well, I've never been in one yet." Adopting my best Rain Man voice, "I'm an excewent dwiver."

"Sure, but nobody's immune. And even if it's the *other* guy's fault, your insurance company will certainly avoid paying because you don't have a French driver's license. You'll be stuck with the bill." So, I was paying insurance premiums, and I wasn't covered?

I've never known insurance companies to look after my best interest. French insurers are simply moreso. If you have a car accident, your French insurance company proposes a lowball offer, and you refuse, telling them to make it better, they have the right to exonerate themselves completely from any reimbursement.

It must be said that the French LOVE insurance. What's their favorite investment? Life insurance; 85% of the population has a policy. Who's the biggest insurance company in the world? AXA - French. The French take out insurance for everything.

Want to send your kid to school? You must provide proof of insurance in case he steps on another kid's toe. Swim class? Insurance. Play in a tennis club? Insurance. Rent a holiday cabin in the mountains? Insurance. Ski on the slopes? Insurance. In France, even the insurance has insurance.

It's true, the national health insurance, the *Assurance Maladie* (CPAM), covers 70% of most expenses. The other 30% would be called a 'co-pay' or out-of-pocket expense in the United States. Not so in France. Almost all companies mandate that their employees sign up for their firm's supplemental health insurance, called a *mutuelle*. The *mutuelle* covers the remaining 30%. The monthly premium is automatically deducted from your pay. There's no way around it.

I'm not complaining, because the health service in France is excellent, and much less expensive than the 'States. A doctor's visit is only €23 and even that small fee is reimbursed within days. Once I had a house call and an hour-long examination for that price. I've had podiatrists and chiropractors here not charge me for second and third visits, relaying sheepishly that as a professional, they felt they should have fixed the problem for good the first time.

But for most other areas of daily life, the insurance thing is out of hand. Take homeowner's insurance, which we discovered later on when we were able to buy an apartment in France. Back in the 'States, we were also required to take out a policy for our home. After the 20% equity threshold had been reached, we were no longer obliged to carry a policy. We did, of course, but WE decided which company to go through, we decided the amount of coverage, and the beneficiary was us as homeowners.

Not so in France. You must hold a policy until the very last *centime* has been paid on the property. It must cover every possible catastrophe under the sun, and the beneficiary is always the bank. Americans used to free accounts would be appalled to learn that French account holders spent €229 on average in bank fees last year.

Which company do you go through to get this wonderful homeowner's insurance? The bank's. They make it part and parcel of your loan deal, so 85% of homeowners in France are handcuffed to their bank's policy. Won't go through their insurer? No deal.

Recent laws have opened up competition for consumers, but banks are dragging their feet. When they hear you want to go outside for a different insurer, their loan rate suddenly goes up. Or the opposite occurs, a sort of bait-and-switch. "We'll match that other bank's loan rate if you go with our bank and *our insurer.*" You agree, and after undergoing their insurance company's doctor's examination, that cough you had suddenly becomes an asthma risk, shooting your premiums higher than the unbundled rival offer. Bank insurance costs three times as much as outside insurers, representing a massive 30% of the total cost of the loan.

Regardless of my overall aversion to insurance, my worrywart friends got to me, and I didn't want to keep paying for nothing. So, I started looking around for options on getting a French driver's license among the American expat community. Some of them were diplomats, so exempt from the requirement. Others were from South Carolina, with the simple exchange accord in place. Lucky gamecocks.

Very few were regular Joes like me from rogue states like California, Washington or New York. Most were on three-year expat assignments. All of those expats I knew simply chanced it, overstaying the legal requirement by two years and then scurrying onto the next gig in a different country. Some left sooner than that, freaked out by the daunting process. The worst were the spouses, who had no French language knowledge prior to being dragged across the world by their significant other. Several of them pushed their husbands to return early. Among dozens of fellow Yanks in my circle, I didn't know a *single* soul who had undergone the administrative process of obtaining a French permit, much less completed it. In my outer circle, I learned of people who had moved here as long ago as 1994, and still used their old US State license, accepting the risk. I was on my own.

I broke down and signed up with my local French driving school- an '*auto-école*.' At least then if I was pulled over, I could say that I was 'in the process' and trying my darndest to comply, mister ossifer, and blame the delays on someone else.

So, I went down to my local *auto-école*. They claimed that 4 out of 5 of their students passed the first time, which sounded good to me. I discovered later that 63% of schools claim an inaccurate success rate.

They had me fill out the CERFA 02 form, get four photos taken in the right format, submit them with a copy of my ID card, and my original electricity bill not older than three months (proving where I lived). Oh, and five self-addressed stamped envelopes, or SASE as we call them in the 'States. Not any SASE, mind you, but the kind called 'LRAR' here which offered a tracking number and proof of receipt, at €5 a pop. While I gathered these items, the school was very happy to take my initial check. It would be one of many.

Auto-écoles are a big scam costing the candidate €1 800 on average across the land, and a phenomenal €2 140 in Paris. This cost is so prohibitive for young people, that half of them put it off until they can save up the money. It's all private instruction from one of 10 000 certified institutions. The State absolutely loves to slough off the training responsibility to these companies. The government has none of the heavy lifting, while continuing to pocket the 20% VAT. The value-added-taxes alone on driver training contributes €300 million annually to the *gouvernement*.

The industry is big enough to have its own trade conference, The *Driving Instructor Show*, where all the people gather who make money off of students. Nothing happens with public instructors during high school time, like it did in my day. Also, while the government will provide loans, it doesn't subsidize the cost of auto school. This, coming from a country which subsidizes or controls the cost of everything. Books and standard 250-gram baguettes must be sold at the same price everywhere in the land.

More people take the written test for the code each year than the *baccalaureate* final exam for high school graduation. 1 440 000 candidates go through the license exam annually in France. The *auto-écoles* know that every one of those people has to go through them. It's the *auto-écoles* who present candidates for examination, at €130 a pop. If they don't agree that you're up to snuff, you must pay them for more instruction, or more time behind the wheel. At nearly *€55 per hour* of road time, they have a built-in incentive to say you suck at driving. You must spend at least 20 hours of in-car driving instruction with the *auto-école*. They are the gatekeepers to obtain certification necessary to go the *Préfecture* on test day. The *auto-école* has you by the ball-bearings.

This is the system I submitted myself to when I signed up.

CHAPTER EIGHTEEN

Borne 425 - Dwayne, a 3-act tragedy, Act I

Dwayne, partie I

After several incidents where the load capacity of our only vehicle was strained, we began thinking about a bigger car. The Fait Accompli wasn't ideal for moving house, long trips with suitcases or transporting a stroller and all the other crap vital to a toddler's well-being. Parents, you know those things that junior just can't live without? And then three months later it's too small, or of no further pedagogical use? We had all of that, and of course paid full-price to get it new, so our child could be the first to chew on it.

The cheapest solution we saw to our car space

dilemma was to have our old minivan shipped over from Los Angeles for $1 000. Our green Dodge Caravan had served us well back in California for a couple years before moving. The car was a bit lumbering and slow, so my friend, Dave, nicknamed it 'Dwayne' for Dwayne Crutchfield.

In his second year with the Rams, Eric Dickerson shattered the NFL single-season rushing record. So, it stands to reason in their 1984 *playoff game*, with the clock winding down, and Dickerson's team on the opponents' goal-line, when a touchdown wins the game, the Rams gave the ball to... Dwayne Crutchfield. Dwayne, the 1984 football player, didn't score, and his team lost. Dwayne, the 1997 minivan, was certainly the alternative of sleek, stylish and record-setting.

Parked on the street in front of my folks' house, Dwayne wasn't appreciating any. There are so many used cars in Southern California, that they're worth practically nothing. Dwayne was also still costing us in registration and insurance, not to mention the odd parking ticket for wearing out his welcome on the street. Selling in L.A. meant getting about $3 000, almost nothing for the money we paid, then bringing the funds over meant losing 30%, because the exchange rate was $1.30 to €1.

I'd heard horror stories about adapting US cars for EU roads, thus I was hesitant. So, I went looking around US car brand showrooms to see if there were any equivalents. I found it. Marketed here as the "Chrysler *Voyageur*," I saw several examples of our car. Plus, it was advertised in the *Argus*, the reference in France for used cars, at €6 000, more than twice the LA value. After $1 000 for international shipping, we'd still be ahead of the game. The Chrysler *Voyageur* looked identical to my lay eye. I said to myself, "how different can it be?"

My folks drove the Dodge Caravan down to San Pedro to board on a container. It was stuffed to the sunroof with other items, because the transport price is the same full or empty, and we were still within the one-year window to have customs fees waived for a personal move. A month or so later, my wife picked it up from Le Havre.

To start the administrative process, we went down to the *Préfecture*. Sure enough, we were told to have a repair shop see what was needed for Dwayne to conform. Meanwhile, we were free to drive as-is, with California plates. This interim period gave us a short reprieve from administrative hell, and offered an added benefit.

With Dwayne's California plates, we didn't appear on *any* system, neither in France nor anywhere else in Europe, which had likewise seen a proliferation of the picture-snapping radar devils. Pics of Dwayne must have been tossed in the trash, for we never saw any.

We did get radar trapped from time to time in the Fait Accompli with French license plates. 'Ta-da! Here's your ticket!' It was sent to Monsieur, because that was the name on the pink slip. The one unique owner always takes the blame for the traffic offense, regardless of who's actually driving. We'd pay the reduced fine of €45 by responding within the first two weeks and accepting that I was at fault.

Only there was no penalty, no points taken off. Monsieur doesn't exist in the system either. You have to have a French license in order for the French administration to take points away. So now we had two cars, and two drivers, and no matter who drove which car, however fast, we'd never get any points deducted. If we drove the California car, we couldn't even get fines.

Dwayne's lumbering nature kept us under the speed limit a lot of the time. It was such a pleasure to just drive instinctively. We didn't need to constantly look back and forth between forever changing speed limit signs and the speedometer. Imagine not worrying or even thinking about speed. Keep your eyes on the conditions in front of you and react accordingly.

Untouchable behind our California plates, for once the system was screwed up in our favor.

CHAPTER NINETEEN

Borne 450 - Driver's Ed paperwork shuffle

Paperasse de l'auto-école

For the first few months, every other time I walked in to my *auto-école* for practice, they informed me that something *ELSE* was needed on my paperwork.

First, the *Préfecture* sent my file back because the photo didn't have a white background. I had gone to a photo specialist to have a so-called professional snap my portrait. I showed *Monsieur Pro* a copy of the specifications, specifically to avoid this kind of error. I had paid €10 for the French Touch the first time, because I knew the €4 kiosk photos would be rejected. But instead, the Pro pulled down a backdrop with a bit too much grey in it. The second time, the photo shop guy acknowledged the human error... as *mine-* and promptly pocketed another tenner.

A white background photo was submitted to the *auto-école*, along with another registered SASE. The school gathered up all the other new student dossiers and sent them in one bulk package to the *Préfecture*. A couple practice sessions later, the school informed me that the *Préfecture* now wanted to have my California Driver's license translated.

"Why?" I said. "It's not like they're giving me credit for possessing a valid foreign license."

"I dunno," she shrugged. "The *Préfecture* is always asking for these crazy things without notifying you beforehand of what they want. Then, they change the rules, saying y'know, that thing they absolutely *had* to have before? Well, now it's a different thing. They're also extremely slow. Calling them does nothing. We have to go down there regularly and wait in line like some loser to unblock the situation for our students."

Thus began a marathon tennis match in which I was to play the part of the ball. The *auto-école* would point the finger at the *Préfecture* for all delays, errors and omissions. All the while they'd commiserate, looking upon me with blinking understanding eyes, imploring me they were on my side and faultless. When I'd call the *Préfecture* for clarification on a certain request, and reach a human without too much trouble, they'd respond in bewildered fashion that it was my *auto-école*'s job to handle this or that, or at least inform me ahead of time. I didn't know who to believe, but I didn't want to get on anybody's bad side.

I translated all the text on my CA DL myself, and submitted the document. It was returned two weeks later as unsatisfactory. The translator had to be a known authority on the French government's list of approved suppliers. Calls into the first couple names on the list produced quotes well above €200.

"That's more than €10 per word!" I complained. Doesn't matter, they replied, that's our minimum. Take it or leave it.

I left it, and called a translator who worked with the French consulate in San Francisco. For $75 it was done. Not Highway robbery- more like *Départementale* robbery.

The translation was sent off anew, and I went back to my lessons. Again, after two weeks, the file returned to sender.

"They want an original copy of your electricity bill," the bored deskwarmer informed me at the *auto-école*.

"I submitted it," I said puzzled, and reached for the file to point out the document.

"That one's more than three months old," she pre-empted.

"Well, if I'd been told thoroughly about all these requirements in the first place, the file wouldn't have gone back-and-forth for more than three months. Couldn't these requests by the *Préfecture* have been anticipated?"

Ignoring my question, "They need a new one, more recent, which proves you haven't moved."

I brought back the most recent EDF statement the next week, and asked, "Could you please double-check that absolutely everything in my file is complete and meets requirements."

She gave a cursory run-through, about two seconds longer than usual. Looking up with unworried eyes, she invited me to take a grade-school desk in the video room, while she popped another worn cassette in the machine.

Bright and early one morning, the *Préfecture* wrote upon it, 'return to sender.' This time it was rejected because the photo had a *white* background. "But that's what they asked for!" my head screamed. After several years, the administration had changed their requirements. Now, all driver's license photos needed to have a blue background.

The staff at the photo place must have wondered if I wasn't full of myself, getting all these pro selfies taken. This time, I anticipated the runaround about my address, and submitted the pix along with that month's electricity bill.

My CERFA 02 file completed six round-trips to the Préfecture and back to the *auto-école*. I didn't know at the time, but that was just the beginning. My dossier would become as well-travelled as that garden gnome in *Le Fabuleux Destin d'Amélie Poulain*.

CHAPTER TWENTY

Borne 475 - Moving with McQueen

Déménagement avec McQueen

In mid-2005, we decided we didn't want to spend another Winter in the drafty *maison de gardien*. Plus, in the cold months, it became a bit crowded with all the weasels and other rodents scurrying into the attic.

So, we went home shopping. After realizing that buying a house was out of our price range, we settled on an apartment. After dozens of visits, *Madame's* impossible requirements of a fireplace and garden were surprisingly met in a flat we found built in the 1960s. I just wanted to be close to a train station, and we got that too, near the gare de Saint-Nom-la-Bretèche.

Home transactions move slower here. We first visited our future apartment when the fragrant purple wisteria was in bloom in the garden. By the time we took possession, it was below freezing. This produced a moving experience we didn't anticipate.

It had been hovering around zero celsius for a week. We had celebrated a crisp Thanksgiving just two days earlier. The ground was dry, but the Saturday morning clouds looked ominous. The moving van was already rented and four hardy men in work clothes were at the go. Well, three men looking like dock workers, and Anselm, who had shown up in slacks and dress shoes. We started to load up in Le Vésinet.

When the truck was about half-full, the first drop of moisture hit my nose. "This is really early for the first snow" I said, thinking it would melt upon first contact with the ground. It didn't, and it kept falling fast. By the time we were packed and on our way, there were a couple of inches on the ground. No worries, as we were gripping the flat Le Vésinet road OK.

As we approached the new village, the road began to slope gradually up, and I felt a little slippage behind the steering wheel. I slowed and the tires held all right until we arrived at the foot of the new street, a one-way circle. I hadn't before realized that our new home was uphill. The climb went counter-clockwise up all the way until 12 o'clock. Our front gate was at 10 o'clock, the beginning of the downward slope. In low gear, I gave us some momentum in the direction of 5 o'clock. At a 5% grade, my rear-wheel drive truck's tires spun into nothingness. It was just too steep. After several attempts, I was forced to park, about two football field's distance downhill from our front door.

We couldn't go on and we couldn't go back. Our former home was already rented and the new tenants would move in tomorrow. That is, if we could get the second half of our stuff removed by then. The snow continued to fall, along with my hopes.

With my bed packed in the back, where would I sleep? Would the van rental company let me use the thing another day? If so, would they charge me triple, since they were closed on Sunday? My brother-in-law Philippe had traveled up from Limousin to help us move. Did he come four hours on the train for nothing? All my extra hands would be back to their regular jobs on Monday. I'd have to take the day off and move everything myself. Was I even capable of that?

Then, I remembered at a meeting of the homeowner's association, it was mentioned that some neighbors kept road salt. We started knocking on doors and got two bags. We scattered too lightly along about 40 yards. I knew it'd never be enough.

Anselm's loafers slid on the snowy street and he slipped onto his slacks. He got up to show his wet bottom. Our desperation was complete.

Flakes continued to float down. A neighbor's head peeked out, then another. The last grains of our bags dropped out at the bottom of the hill, near the moving van. We headed back up the street for our only shovel.

Rounding the bend, we saw about a dozen comrades and kids clearing the road, pouring three more bags of salt! At the same time, the snow had halted, and we could begin to see the asphalt in some places. The community was pitching in, and somebody up there was cooperating. A glint of hope, George Bailey style, began to rise in me.

My buddy Jean-Pierre from the moving crew, who was more used to driving in the snow than this Cali boy, said now was the time. He had analyzed the situation and deduced that there was only one way to get the moving van up to my place: backwards. He'd be driving blind up the wrong direction of the one-way road. Before I could protest, he had taken the wheel and turned the truck around.

We spotted him on either side, to guide him or nudge the truck. Sure enough, with most of the weight off the back tires, the backwards truck started gripping like a front-wheel-drive. The initial attempt was promising, and we were making slow progress. There were two corners where the van stalled, and we narrowly avoided parked cars. The truck was now positioned at 7 o'clock, with its rear pointed toward the uphill straightaway. We held, and pushed until the wheels caught. That was all the signal Jean-Pierre needed and he shot all the way up the hill.

The ground crew was euphoric! Until we thought, "Hey, he can't see any oncoming cars. How's he going to stop? How's he going to turn?" We ran up the hill after him. From a distance, we saw him execute a maneuver right out of an action film. Rather than putting on the brakes at his destination, Jean-Pierre merely let off the gas, and at the perfect moment, jack-knifed the truck until it slid perpendicular to the road, coming to rest dead in front of our gate. He had maybe three feet of clearance before either bumper. Jean-Pierre McQueen.

Unrolling the back of the van, we found all of our goods intact. We unloaded in a cheerful mood and celebrated with Goudale beer and cold cuts.

Our first move in France was during a heat wave. We'd now come full-circle, moving in the snowfall.

CHAPTER TWENTY-ONE

Borne 500 - Driver's Ed - in the classroom

Auto-école salle d'instruction

The main service my driving school provided consisted of a small decrepit room with 10 middle school desks, a solid state TV monitor and a 1980s VCR. The instructor would press play, a random quiz of 40 questions would be shown, and 30 minutes later, they'd tabulate scores. The instructor would answer a few questions if asked, press play, then go back to another 30-minute smoke break. The only time I saw them not warming their desk chair was to exchange a tape, or *fume une clope*.

I'd usually have many questions for them at first, because there was a lot I didn't understand. Like, "how do you answer the multiple-choice ones?" I know, it sounds like a stupid question, because my American public-school education was filled with multiple-choice tests. I had way more scantrons with number two pencils than essays or long-form responses. A, B, C or D? Sometimes all of the above. Sometimes, none of the above. That part I got.

But the French code questions were only half of the time A/B/C/D, and the other half was split up into TWO queries inside EACH question. For example: Part 1, answer A or B; Part 2 answer C or D. If you got *either* part wrong, the *whole* answer was wrong.

Fifty percent of the questions were two-parters. So, 20 of the questions required 40 correct answers. This meant that the minimum passing score wasn't really 35 out of 40. In fact, to pass, you have to check at least 53 right responses out of 40 questions!

Here are some examples of these double-jeopardy questions-

At the next intersection, I will yield to vehicles coming from the:

-right	*YES*	____*A*	*NO*	____*B*
-left	*YES*	____*C*	*NO*	____*D*

This sign indicates a lane reserved for:

-cyclists	*YES*	____*A*	*NO*	____*B*
-cyclomotorists	*YES*	____*C*	*NO*	____*D*

If you're wondering, "what's a '*cyclomotor*,'" so was I. The *auto école* lady answered helpfully, "It's like a *mobylette*, what." I found out it's not a scooter, per se, but everyone calls it a scooter, and every other two-wheeler with a motor and no clutch is designated on the street by the name, 'scooter.' The test distinguishes three kinds of scooters: under 50cc's (or *cyclomotor* by legal definition), between 50cc's and 125cc's, and above 125cc's. You need to become an expert in the wide variety of two-wheeled motorized transportation devices.

Here's another fun one:

It's raining. I can drive:
90 km/h _____A
100 km/h _____B
110 km/h _____C
130 km/h _____D

Did you answer 'A, B and C?' Neither did I. I knew the limit was 110 kilometers per hour on that stretch of road, but I wasn't going to include ALL the different speeds *below* that. I CAN drive... 87.34 km/h. I could have left everything blank, showing I CAN drive... not at all. I have choices, you know. I CAN drive... in a purple shirt listening to the Osmonds on 8-track. I don't have to be pigeonholed into three measly possibilities among thousands of legal ones.

Speaking of legal, as a citizen of any country, you're supposed to know what you may and may not do. Do your taxes, and don't steal, for example. You can't say 'nobody told me I couldn't steal.' Ignorance of the law is no excuse. I get it.

However, US citizens aren't expected to know the *penalty* for ALL forms of stealing, are they? What if I steal a candy bar from a convenience store? What if I steal 1 000 candy bars? How about if I steal 1 000 candy bars at gunpoint? And take the 1 000 candy bars across the state line, what then? Lawyers and judges are supposed to know these things, but regular folks need know only *do* it, or *don't* do it.

Not so French drivers. They're expected to have lawyer-level knowledge of the implications for messing up on the road. Here's a sample *question* of the genre:

If I don't obey a street traffic policeman telling me to stop, I risk:
-a fine of 3 750 euros　　　*YES____A*　　　*NO____B*
-a loss of 6 points　　　　*YES____C*　　　*NO____D*

Speaking of gestures, do you know *how* a gendarme signals a motorist to pull over? Me neither. None of the code books cover this essential aspect. There are zero pictograms or photos of officers motioning to drivers. I know that flashing lights and sirens on the cop car behind me mean I should slow and move to the right. If they persist behind my bumper, then I should stop completely beside the road. I learned that in the 'States, and the same applies here. However, the French road police almost *NEVER* pull over folks that way.

It's comical now, looking back at OJ's Ford Bronco chased by patrolmen and helicopters for hours on the LA freeways. Such chases are repeated routinely to this day on US shows like Cops. That simply doesn't happen in France. If they want to stop a driver, they'll simply block the exits (what few ones there are) and barricade the freeway. In less than 10 miles, the chase is over.

When police want to create a checkpoint, they stand in threes by the side of the road, with their hands behind their backs. Officers I've seen in this formation have never waved as much as a hello to me, so how am I to know if they want me to pull over? Do they hold up their hand like a stop sign, or point to the place where they want me to pull over? Do they make an L with their arms? Or maybe it's other letters, like Y-M-C-A? Do they perform Tecktonik? I know the signals by heart for pass interference, holding and unnecessary roughness. You'd think the pull over sign would be more universal than American football penalties.

You're also expected to know about technological innovations, which only appear on some cars.

My vehicle is equipped with the eCall urgent phoning system:
-it is geolocalized
YES _____A   NO   _____B
-emergency services are automatically called in the case of an accident
YES _____ C   NO   _____D
Oh, yeah? Well my friend Tai has the car horn jingle system installed. Riddle me this- True or False: Offenbach's *French Can-Can* is included.

Needless to say, my initial scores from trial tests were in the teens. It was going to take me a lot longer than I thought to prepare for the written test. It didn't help that my *auto-école* was only open afternoons Wednesday, Friday and Saturday. That's when most high-schoolers were out of class. I was the only working adult in my school, and they weren't going to change their hours for me. That meant I could only go on the weekends, just a couple hours each week. This I did for months upon months upon months.

On a half-dozen occasions, the school was closed. Either the one employee was sick, or giving a lesson on the road. Sometimes we wouldn't know why. Three or four of us would mull around outside for about 20 minutes before giving up. The other young students complained that there wasn't another bus for an hour. I'd hop in my car and drive off to astonished looks.

CHAPTER TWENTY-TWO

Borne 525 - Surprise underground

Souterraine surprise

For three days, we were doing it like the bears in the woods...

"You've got to come home from work NOW!" My wife was insistant. "We can't let the upstairs neighbor to all the work."
"What work? What are you talking about?"
"He's digging down to the septic tank."
"We have a septic tank? The previous owners didn't say anything about that. I thought it all went to the street sewers."

"The plumber was here, and that problem we've been having with flushing, he says we probably have a sceptic tank. And it must be full. We have to clear it out. But first we have to find it."

I hurried home in my business suit, wondering what I'd find when I got there. I jog-walked from the train station in the crisp -1° night. At least it wasn't snowing.

There were floodlights all over the driveway. Alain, from the upstairs apartment, was up to his knees in a ditch leading from the house out to the garden. He had gotten down to the pipe, and was now following it out toward the street. I quickly changed and grabbed my shovel to join him in the hunt for the tank.

About 15 feet from the building, we found it. It was a really weird setup. The pipe led to the tank, which led to the street. Technically, we *were* connected with the sewers, but not before the sludge filled up the tank. The heavier junk fell to the bottom, and never came out.

Something in the outgoing pipe was blocked. The week prior, it took a long time for the toilets to flush. Then, it wouldn't go down at all. Lately, it was overflowing in the apartment, which led us to call the plumber. Need I describe the stench?

The top of the tank was lifted off, and the problems were easy to see. The former owners had stuck all manner of things down their toilet. There were diapers, and rags, and feminine hygiene thingies clogging the outgoing pipe. Alain got a stick and with several pokes, started the outbound flow anew. It was no longer overflowing, but remained full. The previous owners were kind enough to leave us more than 1 000 liters of backed-up untreated septic tank!

We spent another night without toilets or showers. The next day, the wives got a company to come out and clear the sludge. It was only a temporary solution. Soon the tank would fill up again. Alain found another plumber who would work '*au black*,' meaning accept payment under the table. It still cost €1 000 split two ways to drain the tank anew, connect the pipes directly to the sewers, and fill the empty tank with sand.

As if that wasn't bad enough, the building had another smelly underground tank had to be looked after. The heating oil for our apartment complex is stored in a tank in the backyard, not far from the furnace. There is no connection to the city gas. The heating oil reservoir didn't have a working fuel gauge. Guess how we found out that there was no more oil? That's right, another sub-freezing evening when the radiators all went cold.

The delivery company said they'd be happy to schedule an appointment in a week for the regular price. Or, they could come out that same day for a higher price. We ordered their minimum 2 000 liters for same-day service. From then on, it was my job once a month to put a stick down the oil tank, and see if we needed to order.

Thankfully, after all the emergency repairs and fillups, we still had a bit of money left over. It was necessary because the kitchen consisted of an old basin. That's it. No stove. No fridge. No cupboards or counters. This wasn't a barn we were trying to reconvert. It was an apartment in a structure built in the 1960s in a modern residential lot. Still, it needed a complete kitchen. We decided to put in new flooring and paint as well. Enter Strong and North.

Aurore had found some artisans through friends

who had work done on their house. Paul overheard her confirming an appointment with *Monsieur LeFort* for the next day. "Can I meet him, *Maman*?"

"Of course, my little flea," she said. He went into his room to play with Mr. Incredible, Action Man, and his other figurines, imagining what Mister Strong must be like. Coming home from school, he found out.

Monsieur LeFort was only slightly taller than Paul, who was in primary school. He tried to hide his deception by holding his tongue, but his open-mouthed gape said all. "Surprising, eh?" said Monsieur LeFort, playing along.

One of his crew members liked to sing while working. He'd belt out "*Au Nord...*" let the sound trail off, and continue laying floorboards. Every couple of minutes, he'd repeat his chorus, or rather the start of a chorus. "*Auu Nooord...*" he'd begin again. None of us could recognize the song. We knew the words meant 'in the North,' but *what* exactly is in the North? "*Auuu Nooooord...*" Two words. Two notes. In a foreign language. It was like the most impossible round ever of Name That Tune.

We got tired of guessing and asked another member of the crew what song it was.

"I have no idea. That's all he ever sings."

None of them knew. They even nicknamed him '*Au Nord*.' It was all friendly banter, and *Au Nord* was a happy-go-lucky guy. We couldn't ask North himself, because those two words were the only thing we ever understood coming out of his mouth.

Aurore would struggle to comprehend when North would engage her in conversation. "I'm sorry, I didn't quite get that." "Could you repeat, please?" "Come again?" "Must be the noise of the machines." She tried every form of politeness she knew but further repeating didn't help. Mister LeFort would step in and translate, asking if he should do the floor this way or that.

Many years later, I was driving a friend home, when it finally came on the radio. I jerked the steering wheel, startled by the familiar refrain.

"What was that? Are you OK?" asked Stéphane.

"Yeah, it's just that, a long, lost mystery is about to be solved."

He didn't know the song either, so we sat there in silence waiting for the end, and the announcement of singer and song. But the station played another one back-to-back. So, I explained about our worker, and how my '*au nord*' search turned up nothing on the internet. It must not have been the name of the number. After a third song, the DJ gave a recap of all that came before, and we finally learned that Pierre Bachelet sang '*Les Corons.*' In the North... there are coal mines.

"Everybody knows that," said Stéphane.

The following Spring, the *mairie* organized a village-wide '*vide grenier.*' It's 'empty your attic' instead of a yard sale, which isn't done on an individual level. No, once a year, the *marché* lot is taken over by all the residents looking to get rid of their junk. I thought it would be a good way to get to know the community, so I took a 10' x 10' space, and paid €10 to sit there for 10 hours. My sales that day barely recouped my initial investment. You see, our mayor doesn't like to advertise, so nobody from out-of-town knows that our little attic sale is taking place. So, instead of finding a happy home far from here, we exchange our burdens with the lady down the street. Our crap simply moves a few doors down. There's more barter than money changing hands.

That evening, people give up trying to sell their junk, and just haul it back in front of their house for anyone to take. The board games, chairs and stuffed animals are scorned one last time before ending up in the '*encombrant*' truck.

French neighborhoods have a system for picking up *encombrants*, or larger items that you no longer want, but don't fit in the trash. These could be old tables, or washing machines, or metal scraps, really anything laying around that you don't want anymore. Instead of taking them to the dump, the last Monday of the month, the city sends a truck by to pick them up.

As one person's trash is another's treasure, these piles on the sidewalk are picked through by bargain hunters swooping in from far away. Every last Sunday of the month, we'd see beat-up white vans by the dozen drive slowly by our street. You know the kind of van the killer used in Silence of the Lambs? That van. Dozens of that van.

Apparently that Summer, I didn't have enough challenges in my life, so I decided to build a woodshed in the garden. I anticipated my biggest issue would be with metric measures. So, I prepared myself by converting 2 x 4 (inches) into 5 x 10 (centimeters) and so forth on my designs. Turns out the dimensions for hardware store items aren't listed in centimeters, but millimeters. So, the 5cm x 10cm board I wanted would be labeled 50mm x 100mm. OK, fair enough, but where *is* it?

I drove to my local Castorama to look for lumber matching these dimensions. I was prepared to settle for boards that were close enough to my plans, but not exactly. It's a woodshed, after all, not stairs, or something where safety is important. What I didn't expect was another vocabulary lesson.

You see, in France, each type of board has a name all its own. The name carries with it a dimension and a purpose. There are no two by fours, nor four by fours. Here, those each have a distinct name.

Arriving at Castorama's drive-thru outdoor lumber yard, I would have been better off with a Bescherelle dictionary than a tape measure. I saw signs for roofing lumber, kits for decorative gazebos, and special cuts for fabricating shutters. There was nothing showing regular boys' outdoor wood for creative projects like mine. I had a case of the hardware woes.

"Excuse-me," I asked a passing worker on a forklift, "I'm looking to build a shed to keep firewood. Where can I find the boards I need?"

"Well, behind you there's the *madriers*, the *bastaings* and *chevrons* for building the roof frame of a house."

"Those are all too thick and heavy for the top, but maybe I could use some for the sides, or the bottom."

"It's only Class 2 wood, and it will rot in the rain. It needs to have tiles over it to keep it dry."

"Sounds like I need something else, especially for the floor."

"Do you mean *lambourdes*?"

"I don't know what those are."

"That's Class 4 wood you could leave outside all year. You'll find them in the garden section."

Walking to the other extremity of the store, I stumbled upon the *lambourdes*. They were too thin to be posts, but could work around the bottom if I got enough of them. I couldn't find any store personnel outside, so I went back in to look for long square boards for the corners. There was an aisle with doors, and right next to them, these huge 6" x 6" posts, but they had notches carved out all along the four edges. I didn't care aesthetically, but asked a blue and yellow shirt if the notches would compromise their ability to hold up a roof.

"They're for a ceiling, not for a roof. That's a *poutre*. What you want is a *poteau*. They're outside with the fencing material."

Sure enough, there were posts, next to ready-made panels with half-moon tops to make a fence. They had grooves cut into them to easily slide the fixed-sized panel in-between the posts. So everybody here used the same legos to enclose their yard? With the extreme variances in the dimensions of properties, I found that hard to believe. Yet, I'd never seen a 'half' panel standing out like a sore thumb. Maybe they arbitrarily decided to retract or expand their space to accomodate the entire panel.

So, I had my floorboards and posts. Now I needed some strips of wood for the outside skeleton. Nothing structural, just good enough to hang some covering for the walls. These, I was told, would be found inside, by the indoor decorative wood aisle. All the indoor stuff is strictly Class 1, so I'd have to treat everything with several coats of fungicide or it wouldn't last one Winter. The strips were called *liteau* if they were square, *tasseau* for rectangular or *chanlatte* for triangular. I opted for the rectangular, which were the easiest to screw into the frame. Nobody would see them, because the covering would hide the skeleton underneath.

At this point, I was pretty tired of the run-around, but I still needed wood for the roof. I hadn't seen any flat sheets at either outside section. So, I asked a helper inside the best I knew how.

"Uh, hi, I need to make a flat roof, so I need some wood. Where could I find a *feuille*, I mean a *carreau*, well, square or rectangular wood, a bit bigger than two meters by two meters."

"I can't help you unless you're clear about what you want. Do you want a *tablette*, or a *panneau*, or a *plaque*, or..."

"*Laissez tomber.* Forget it. I think I have some scraps lying around that I can re-use."

Sure enough, there was an IKEA closet that had disintegrated in the move. Their stuff is only made to be put together once, if that. I cut up the particle board sheets and staggered them on an incline. Covering them with tar roofing shingles made a serviceable roof. Putting it all together took almost less time than finding the parts.

I had built my first permanent structure in my new country. Whatever the outcome of my battles with bureaucracy, if I was kicked out of France now, at least one of my creations would remain.

CHAPTER TWENTY-THREE

Borne 550 - Dwayne, Act II

Dwayne partie II

We weren't in any hurry to make Dwayne compliant. The status quo was suiting us just fine. No muss, no fuss, no tickets.

Sure enough, after about a year the administration sent us a letter. The gist was, "Hey guys, you haven't followed-up on your request to make your US car French-road-ready. Don't you want us any more? If we don't hear from you within 15 days, we'll assume you've abandoned the attempt to get your foreign car up to snuff." Our soccer Mom minivan would become an outlaw.

We wrote back that we were 'working on it.' That

bought us another six months. We begrudgingly dragged Dwayne down to the dealership, asking them to calculate the cost of a facelift. A couple days later they came back with the damage: more than €2 000. We couldn't believe it. "Two thousand for those measley modifications?" That bill plus the shipping would eat up all the advantage of having the car over here instead of over there.

Would the dealership buy Dwayne, or accept the car as a trade-in? They wouldn't give the book value, and wouldn't transact until the car met norms. Could they just sell me the parts and I'd install them myself? It would cost about the same, and I'd still need an affidavit from a third-party saying that the work had been done. There didn't seem to be any way around it. Or was there?

I explored other options, like selling Dwayne to a diplomatic family. After all, diplomats had their cars shipped over from the 'States by their US government employer and didn't need to adapt them, as long as they stayed less than three years. I didn't find any takers. Most had their transportation situation squared away.

Those who could have been interested were hit hard by the exchange rate. Their salary was in US Dollars, but all their expenses were in Euros. During that time, the Euro climbed to $1.60, making their cost of living much higher than back home.

To add insult to injury, their work schedule was around US holidays, about half the number of days on the French calendar. This meant that, in the month of May alone, they had to work a week more than the locals. When their kids were out of school for French holidays, and they needed to handle their care at their own expense.

We decided to do some belt-tightening of our own,

and saved up to pimp our ride. The dealership kept the car for three weeks while it was becoming Frenchified. Headlights and tail-lights were switched out, as well as the corresponding knobs on the dash. We now had a new 'fog lamp' setting, for front AND back. Basically, it just made the rear red lights a bit brighter, if you could find out how to turn them on.

When it was done, you wouldn't have noticed any difference. The make-over was a complete farce. The speedometer now showed kilometers. Other than that, the new *Duaîne* was just like the old Dwayne.

Certificate in hand, bill paid and wallet with a blazing hole in it, we drove off to get the minivan inspected by the powers that be. They of course scheduled the look-see at a rendez-vous point an hour's drive from our home, in the middle of the work week, at an inconvenient time, forcing another personal day off. This time at least, it wasn't for nothing, and Dwayne passed muster. Yet another certificate was given, which we could take down to the *Préfecture* to get our *carte grise* (pink slip). We were given a bit more time to have a French license plate stamped out, and we planned on milking the grace period as long as we could.

Soon after Dwayne was officially tagged, we learned visitors were coming for Christmas. My parents would fly over, with my oldest nephew, Mitchell, in tow. It would be his first trip outside the 'States, and we wanted to make it special. He was an avid snowboarder, so we planned to go to the Alps. Well, we'd blown all this cash on Dwayne; might as well get good use out of him transporting six people and gear on an eight-hour trip up to the mountains.

But the wife didn't like the look of the tires. They

weren't bald by any means. In fact, they had about half of their expected lifetime miles yet to roll. However, they weren't adapted to winter in the mountains. Not knowing what weather or conditions we'd hit up there, we bit the bullet and replaced all four tires. On top of that, we bought a new set of chains. All told, we were set back €700. At this rate, Dwayne's makeover would leave us just enough cash to ride down the snow run on an upturned trash can lid.

It turned out there was no cause for worry about the tires nor justification for the extra expense. The surface of the road remained completely snow-free all the way up and back that week.

The cupboards of our weeklong apartment rental were similarly bare. There were no sheets nor towels. Not a single square of toilet paper. No condiments, not even one grain of salt. Zero books. Zilch on board games. All appliances were carefully removed or locked away prior to our arrival. The only exception was an old TV with an aerial. Mind you, this was a nicely kept, centrally situated 3-bedroom apartment that we were paying €1 500 for. The owner obviously had money, but was a cheapskate on amenities and excessively paranoid about being robbed.

In France, you're often seen as guilty before being proven innocent. My son came back from his first day at middle school with a new booklet handed out by his homeroom teacher. I was flabbergasted to discover five pages at the end, each with 10 pre-printed forms, ready to use and tear out, all for the expressed use of reprimanding him for the offenses they were sure he would commit in class. All the students got the detention-ready forms. None of the books had any space for commendations. No praise was expected to be necessary.

Sure enough, the first week, he had three 'crosses' for minor offenses. He was the same kid as he was in Primary school two months prior. But now, his opinion of himself changed. He became more withdrawn and suspicious around authority. One of his friends took the opposite tack, overtly trying to collect as many crosses as possible. He ran out of forms and was onto his second book before his parents clamped down.

This restrictive attitude shows itself often on French roads. In the US, signs abound telling you what you can and can't do. This is annoying and overbearing, but at least informative instead of pre-emptive. In France, you're outright barred from attempting anything seen as untoward. Instead of curbs painted red to warn you away, metal poles and cement blocks ensure parking there is impossible. The entrances to nearly all shopping center parking lots have a metal arch installed, barring all vehicles over two meters tall from entering. They're designed to keep out camping cars from parking overnight, but they also prevent RV folks from shopping there during opening hours. These arches make it impossible for most bicycles on hatchback bike racks from entering (repairs) or exiting (new purchases). Thanks Decathlon! And don't expect to load up your roof rack cargo container with groceries for your camping trip. Thanks Carrefour!

The ski trip went off without a hitch, until it was time to go. We had taken Timinou the cat to the Alps with us for the week. The last day, she decided to hide. All six of us in the cabin couldn't find her anywhere. We didn't have any photos of her, as this was before most phones had cameras, and nobody had Pinterest. So we found a gag postcard with a cat of her breed- on skis with a Santa hat-

and put our number on it. We circulated that around the village and finally attached it to a telephone pole, because it was time to go.

We ended up leaving without the cat. We left word and asked if the property manager could watch for her. Sure enough, halfway to Paris we got a call that the next vacationers, who arrived at the rental hours after we left, found her hiding in a drawer under a bed! We had checked that, I thought. Yes, but what we hadn't counted on was that she would jump out as the drawer was opened, and jump back in as the drawer closed.

Aurore took the train the next weekend to pick up the wayward cat.

CHAPTER TWENTY-FOUR

Borne 575 - Vocabulary

Vocabulaire

When you go through the driver's handbook and videos, you learn all sorts of neat French terms. None of these will be of any use to you in daily life. Most French people learn them also during the code, and drop them immediately after having passed the test. You won't see these words in books by Zola, nor Hugo, nor Dumas. Neither Chevalier nor Trenet nor Piaf sung about them. There's no '*La vie en chaussée.*'

Chaussée is one word found only in the guide. You never hear it spoken on the street- which is where the *chaussée* should be found, if you could find it. Nobody says "park on the opposite side of the *chaussée*." Or, "I crossed the *chaussée* to buy a baguette." Or, that "I saw a dead rabbit in the *chaussée*."

Could the *chaussée* be the lane? Or perhaps all of the lanes going in one direction? Is it the whole road going in both directions? Does it include the bike lane? The shoulder? These words all have equivalents in French, and they're heard all the time in both languages, but not *chaussée*. *Chaussée* is strictly for the test.

In French roundabouts, we drive '*dans le sens inverse des aiguilles d'une montre.*' In English we say 'counter-clockwise.' It's another phrase which takes much longer to say in French than English. Take any 100-page book in English, and the French translation will be 20 pages longer.

There are two kinds of roundabouts, the '*rond point,*' which is actually rarer, and the '*carrefour à sens giratoire,*' which is the normal one you'll encounter 99.9% of the time. It makes sense that the common one is called the *carrefour à sens giratoire*, doesn't it? Really rolls off the tongue like butter. In the '*giratoire*' cars entering must yield to cars already in the '*carrefour,*' but once engaged, they have the priority to get out. For the '*rond point,*' cars entering have the right of way, but they must yield to cars coming in from their right.

This happens at l'Etoile, the roundabout circling the Arc de Triomphe. On that one roundabout 12 roads converge, and all 12 have the right of way over the vehicles already stuck inside. It's very easy to get into, but tough to get out of. The trick is to head straight for the center. Most drivers avoid this. They want to stay as close as they can to the exterior rim, so they won't miss their turnoff street. As a result, they're halted constantly by the flow of incoming traffic, and it takes them forever, in very stressful tight quarters. In the elevated center, there's more room, cars flow and you can actually see the road you want to merge into. You wait just before the street in front of it, and when there's an opening, you zip through. Cars flow into the Etoile like schools of fish because the lights allow them in that way, so there are rarely staggered vehicles, and often clear openings.

Before attending driving school, everybody calls them 'roundabouts.' After obtaining their license, everybody again calls them 'roundabouts.' But during the code everybody has to use the word '*giratoire*' which is unheard of on the street. It would be illogical to call it a '*carrefour à sens giratoire*' anyway, because a *carrefour* is literally a four-sided square. The Code people are trying to fit a square peg in a round hole.

So, learning the vocabulary in the code is about as useful as learning Latin. No, Latin can actually be used to decipher words in Italian, Spanish and other romance languages. The vocabulary in the code can be re-purposed for nothing.

Or maybe one thing: getting directions to a wild party thrown by a group of fun-loving driving instructors and examiners...

Ring, ring
"Hello Adeline, I am quite keen to access your festival this evening."

"Likewise, Bernard. It is quite foggy tonight, so watch out for livestock on the *chaussée*. I hope your tourism vehicle is equipped with fog lights front and rear."

"Naturally. Furthermore, I will keep my Class B permit, which allows me to drive a tourism vehicle, on my person in case the *gendarmes* make a *contrôle*. Is it an important itinerary?"

"Yes, you will take the *Nationale* and *Départemental* all the way. When you arrive, you may park on the *accotement*."

"Are you referring to the *bas côté*?"

"Same thing. Do you know how to get here?"

"No, can you please provide me with the indications to your *agglomeration*?"

"Actually, it's not an *agglomeration*, it's a locality, called '*lieu-dit* L'Extase.' As you're coming from Beaufou, you start off direction Folles, until you see Bellebrune. At the *carrefour à sens giratoire* you take the second exit, go over Monteton and continue down toward Poil. Just after the fork where Le Quiou touches Montcuq you come to L'Extase."

"I'm sure we'll have as much fun as your last party in Bourré."

Click.

CHAPTER TWENTY-FIVE
Borne 600 - Math

Maths

The French love math, which here is called *'maths.'* The extra 's' is for 'superfluous.'

Yes, you can have 1 maths problem. I'm aware the British are poisoned with this affliction as well. However in France, you can also have 1 cookies, 1 muffins and 1 cupcakes!

While the French are not all that great at singular and plural in words borrowed from the English language, they're very good at math. Do you know which French people love math the most? *Fonctionnaires.*

So it's no wonder that calculations are a part of the

Code de la route. This being the land of Descartes, you know you're going to have to do some math.

In the 'States, we like rules of thumb. Leave two seconds between you and the car in front of you to be on the safe side. Anybody can count to two. Not everybody can calculate the stopping distance of a vehicle moving at 90 km/h, even if they're given that the quick formula is to multiply the first digit by itself, then factor in a coefficient of 0.8 for a dry road and 0.4 for a wet road. And those who CAN do that calculation cannot do it in two seconds. This is a real question on the French code.

Or the rule of thumb for alcohol in the 'States: one drink per hour or less, and you're probably under the legal limit. More, and you should stop drinking and wait out the number of hours until they match the number of drinks.

What should you do in France? Get out your slide rule. Better yet, get two of them. You're going to need both because it's not enough to calculate the volume of alcohol in the BLOOD, measured in *grams* per liter. You'll also need to know the amount of alcohol in the BREATH, measured in *milligrams* per liter. Both calculations will be on the test.

You'll also need to know whether the sum you come up with qualifies as the legal limit, or an infraction, or a felony, and how many points are taken away for each level.

How heavy a load are you allowed to carry? Simple, calculate the PTAC. That's how much your car weighs when empty... plus all the people and stuff in it... and being towed behind it. Everyone knows the exact weight of their car, right? The regular class B license allows up to 3 500 kilograms. The test may have some fun scenarios for you to add up.

Geometry:
The peripheral vision of a driver is approximately:
-180° at a standing stop
YES ____*A*   *NO*   ____*B*
-60° at 80 km/h
YES ____*C*   *NO*   ____*D*

Look around to see if you have a ruler handy. Got it? Good. Look at the smallest unit of measure. What is it? It's 1/16th of an inch, right. Not big, is it?

Well, that's about 1.6 millimeters in metric terms. That's at least how much TWI or tread you must have remaining to be legal. Not 1.4mm. Not 1.5mm. No, 1.6mm and more or your tires aren't allowed to roll. Who, besides a scientist with advanced instruments, can measure a *micro*meter, the space in-between millimeters?

Tire pressure:

Nobody has those little tire inflation gauges in their cars here. You have to go to the gas station to see how many bars are in each tire. French drivers should know that a bar is the equivalent of one kilogram of pressure per centimeter cubed.

Personally, I'd just like to know who invented the brilliant system where the button to add air isn't on the end near the tire valve. No, it's on the machine. You go to the machine, grab the hose, try to attach it to the tire valve, go back to the machine, press the button, the needle tells you the hose isn't clamped on properly, you re-clamp, you re-button press, you re-clamp, you re-button press, the needle starts to climb much higher than the real pressure reading, you let go and wait for the needle to drop down to the real number of bars, it's not enough, you press again, and again until the pressure is just right. Great! One tire done! Now, it's off to grab the hose and place it on the next valve. It's really an exercise machine.

Ratios:

Comparing the maximum speed limit on the *Autoroute*, 130 km/h, with the minimum speed allowed, 60 km/h gives us what? A ratio of 2.17 to 1 you say? An accident waiting to happen, I say. Allowing such speed discrepancies on the same stretch of road is asking for trouble.

Parking:

Driving your car into a parking lot in France is a declaration of war. Civil war. Everything from entering the lot, searching and exiting puts you in direct competition with fellow citizens and the laws of physics. In France, 80% of accidents happen while parking.

Parking spaces in France are way too small. They're supposed to be a minimum of 2.5 meters wide, which is a little over 8 feet. Hardly *any* of the spaces are so wide.

The street parking spaces in my town are barely 2 meters wide which is 6'6". My compact car is 1 meter, 80 centimeters wide, or 5'11". Car width only goes up from my car. Most cars on the road are between 5'11" and 6'6" wide. So, there's seven inches clearance between my car and the parking space line on the ground. If I'm parked in the middle of the space and so is the guy next to me, that doubles the clearance, to 14 inches between the two.

How do you open a 10-inch thick door and a 10-inch thick body front-to-back into the 14-inch space between parked cars without causing damage to yourself or your neighbor? You don't! That's why *all* French cars have door dings, and many *chemises* are missing buttons. It's common to see cars in France which have lost their side-view mirrors, torn off by parking garage walls or posts, or passing motorcycle handlebars, or other side-view mirrors.

Just making it safely into a shopping center parking space is an exploit. No wonder. The lots look like they were designed by Rube Goldberg. To compare and contrast, have a look at the following two maps showing how to get from the main motorway to a parking space nearest your store selling housewares.

Here's how you get from the 405 freeway to Sears at South Coast Plaza in Orange County:

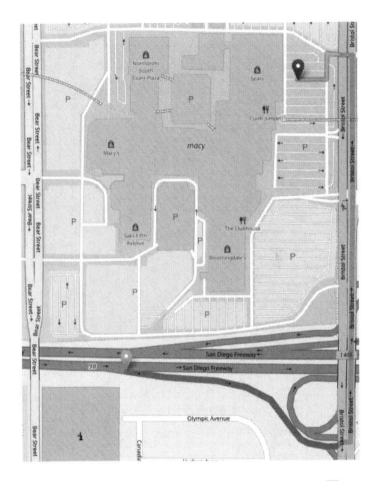

That's four total turns. If you miss one, no biggee. There are at least nine entrances and exits. U-turns on the main streets are possible if you insist on going back to one particular gateway. All surrounding streets are two-way. You can't go wrong.

Now, here's how you get from the Nationale 186 to Habitat at Parly 2 in Le Chesnay:

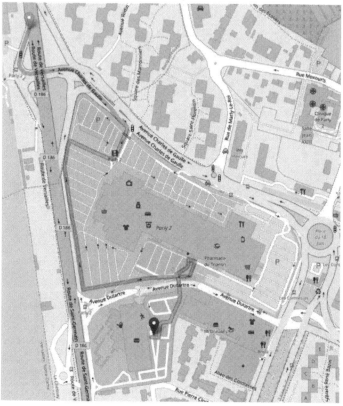

That's 14 turns. If you miss a single one of them, you're in for a world of hurt. One-way streets and dead-ends abound. Parking spots do not, so get to the back of the line. You may have to drive all the way to the beginning and start again, if you can even find your way.

What we usually do in such lots is grab the first open spot we see anywhere in the vicinity, and then walk it. This avoids the driven maze game, but still creates two other issues: 1) how to get there on foot without being killed by moving motorists, and 2) on the way back- how to re-trace our steps to where the car's parked. We've been brought to tears several times from impossible parking structures. The worst had at least three different areas which used the same color-codes and letters. A security guard guided us. "Oh, you're not in *this* Purple E lot, you're in the *other* Purple E lot..."

French mall maps could replace the 'P' sections with the warning 'here be monsters.'

Parking in Paris is a plethora of paradoxes. There are fewer and fewer street parking places in the capital, down 16% in the last 10 years to only 141 000 places. That's one for every 14 residents in the city limits, and one for every four of the 617 000 cars with Paris plates. However, parking revenues have actually increased 66% in the past year. How? Parking fines have been doubled in Paris by the mayor, and enforcement has gone up. Actually, fines were artificially low for years, but the current policy of reducing available spots and hiking rates is putting the pinch on parkers who have fewer legal options.

It's almost impossible to find street parking in Paris. More than 30% of driving time in Paris is spent looking for a parking space. Cars which *are* parked stay way over their welcome. In the month of August, parking is free, so Parisian owners leave their cars, blocking the street spots for out-of-towners. Many of them park '*n'importe comment*,' or 'any which way.' Deliberately parking over the line taking two spots. Blocking exits and entrances to other vehicles. Squeezing right so they can get out their door, but their neighbor's driver's side is completely inaccessible. Examples of such incivility is captured on the website '*garé comme une merde*' or 'parked like a little shit.'

When the meters become active again, many folks don't pay, and ignore the fine when it's sent to their home. Only 15% of Parisians pay their parking tickets (versus 95% of Londoners). With more than four million tickets written annually in Paris, that's a lot of wasted paper. Parisians are used to ignoring parking fines because penalties have been low, and you can accumulate an unlimited number of parking tickets for years. Parkers wait it out, hoping for absolution from above, which surprisingly they often get. Hallelujah!

Routinely when a new administration was elected, parking fines (and sometimes moving violations) have been summarily dismissed as a gift to the populace. This 'presidential amnesty' was last granted by Jacques Chirac in 2002. François Mitterand enacted the amnesty before him, as did Valéry Giscard d'Estaing before him. Bread and circuses, but no new parking spots.

Today's Parisian meter maids use automated terminals which don't leave any notification that your parked car has been ticketed. One writer at *Le Parisien* thought their car was OK for a week. The following week in the mail, they received eight tickets, two from the same day.

That guy was lucky. People in Versailles come back to find no ticket, and NO CAR.

French Presidents like to invite foreign leaders out to Versailles. When they do, streets which routinely accept legal street parking change the rules. Only the municipality doesn't inform the population with notices, cones, barriers and such. They just tow your car to the depot. In March 2017 during a European Summit, 58 cars were towed from Versailles, at the cost to their owners of €245 apiece.

Last *maths* question: How much did that add up to? €14 210 in one day. You can throw a helluva Summit banquet for fourteen G's.

CHAPTER TWENTY-SIX
Borne 625 - Donkey back do-si-do

Dos d'âne do-si-do

The *priorité à droite* takes the *gâteau* for intersection idiocy. However, the left side can be *gauche* in turn. It's when turning left that you encounter the second dumbest road law in France.

Where I'm from, when you turn left at a light, all you need to worry about is the oncoming traffic going straight through the intersection. The oncoming cars turning left pass on my right, as do all the vehicles in the same lane behind it. The two lines of left-turning cars never intersects, traffic flows and the heavens align.

Not so in France. Here, opposing cars turning left

are supposed to pass each other on the left. Picture a square dance with your truck. You roll down your window and arch your left arm out of your pickup. Your partner opposite arrives and you hook elbows. And there you remain while all the other windshield ranchers heading straight dance by you.

Here's what that looks like:

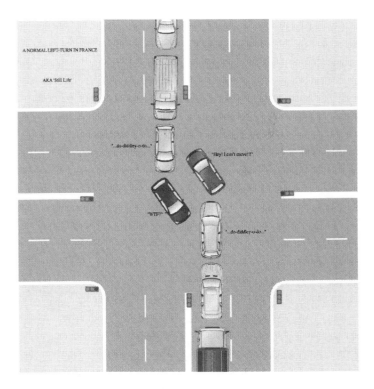

This method bisects the line of traffic – *twice*. I can't move because I'm waiting for Dominique; Dominique can't move because she is waiting for me. And all the left-turning cars behind us in both directions are at a standstill hoping one of us makes a move. What ends up happening is that the light turns red while both of us are stuck in no-man's land. We do-si-do around each other as cross-traffic bears down on us, and grumpy left-turners remain behind in an ever-expanding line.

Some easy flow left-turn intersections *do* exist in France. However they're so rare, and viewed by the locals as so foreign, that they're called 'Indonesian' intersections. Most French drivers are confused when they encounter them.

Not so the Dutch. Indonesia was colonized by the Netherlands, so maybe there's some correlation in how they deal with intersecting roads. Special commendation should be given the Dutch for their ability to drive across complex intersections. The typical crossroads in Holland traverses, in order: two-way pedestrian crosswalks, two-way bike paths, cars from the left, tram tracks from the left, then trams from the right, cars from the right, bikes from both directions, then finally pedestrians from both sides again. Every one of these paths literally has their own light signalling when they can go, which, in the case of the trams may be the same green as you, at a 90° collision trajectory. If both are green, they'd have the right of way, so choose carefully. Driving across a Dutch intersection, you look both ways *seven* times. Traversing in Holland makes me feel like the little frog in that old video arcade game. Frogger must have been invented by a Dutchman. When it comes to intersections, if it ain't Dutch, it ain't much.

Here's an example of one of those wild and crazy 'Indonesian' intersections:

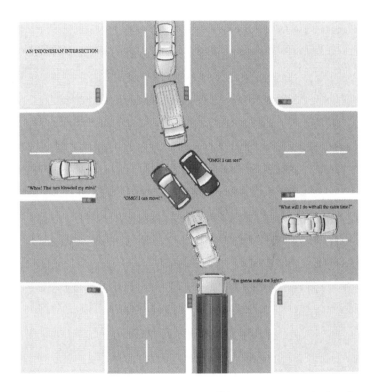

There is another example of a common solution in French road design which posits that the way to avoid accidents is by having lanes deliberately guided into the path of opposing traffic. This is done through the use of *chicanes*, which are obstacles forcing drivers to divert their trajectory. You can see this at the entrance or exit to a village, with such horrors as these: Strategically placed planters in your lane causing you to zigzag; Speed bumps squeezing two-lane roads into one lane over the hump, which can only be crossed by one car at a time. There's a particularly lovely torture chamber I've had the pleasure of navigating often. I'm descending down an incline on a two-lane road bending to the right. A row of mature trees blocks my view of the road ahead, and niftily hides the signs showing the symbols for 'speed bump' and 'yield to oncoming traffic.' You can see neither the bump nor the cars coming from the other direction until you're right on top of them. There I'm confronted with a speed bump and a car on it, squeezed by blocks of concrete on either side at bumper-level. Even driving 20 km/h under the speed limit, I often need to slam on my brakes to avoid French-kissing the oncoming car. Here's what the road looks like after being modified with *chicanes*:

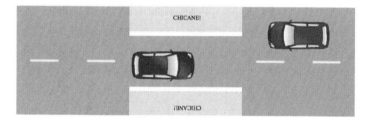

Perfectly suitable and safe roads have been mutilated with these monstrosities. Before, you might have seen the occasional side-scraping. Now, with the modifications, if anything goes wrong, you're guaranteed fatalities from a head-to-head collision.

In addition to the radars, another car-slowing road hazard started springing up like weeds: speed bumps. Called '*dos d'âne*' or 'donkey backs' in French, they were now everywhere. The main road to our town, which previously had only one speed bump, suddenly sprouted 22. Each one was limited to 30 km/h (17 mph). Some were so vicious, even driving over them at the speed limit guaranteed scraping bottom and bumper.

Road works companies had a field day with new jobs pouring out bumps by the boatload. Midas and other sellers of shock absorbers saw their stock rise. Millions of cars, that were doing just fine before, started to develop joint fatigue.

Bumps in Saint-Maur and Montauban were accompanied with speed limit signs of 10 km/h (6 mph)! How is a driver to know if he's even respecting such a low limit since speedometers begin at 20 km/h? One way is to listen for the sound of their plastic bumper cracking, followed by metal scraping asphalt. The speed bump at Montauban has been sculpted and colored so often by passing undercarriages that it resembles a mixed media project by Rodin and Seurat.

The speed bumps really cramped Dwayne's style. Slowing into them wasn't his strong suit. His forward momentum carried him crashing into the front, and bouncing several times on the back end of the bump. Dazed as if leveled by a linebacker, he'd need a moment before revving back up into the flow. He'd barely regain consciousness before being jolted again 100 yards downfield by another bump.

CHAPTER TWENTY-SEVEN

Borne 650 - Dwayne, Act III

Dwayne partie III

The three months following our return from the ski trip became the 'semester of complacency' as far as the minivan was concerned. Dwayne was finally legit, and we didn't need to shuttle around a large group anymore. We could have traded him in for a newer car with less headaches. We could have sold him on the open market. We could have donated his fat ass and gotten a tax write-off.

We did none of these things.

Instead, the following April, I got a panicked call in the early morning from my out-of-breath better half...

"Joe, the Dodge broke down!"

"What? Where?"

Pant, pant. "It won't go. It's stuck." Breath. "I left it in the middle of the road and I'm walking... to work."

"Slow down. Can you stop and catch your breath so I can hear you."

"No time." Pant "I'm going to be late." Pant, pant. "You have to come get it."

"Alright, alright. Just tell me where it is. Where did you leave the car?"

"I don't know. It's on the way." Cough.

"Well, is it closer to work, or closer to home?"

"Work. Maybe Garches. I don't know."

Fait Accompli to the rescue. I hopped in the older 2nd car and headed toward Garches. Luckily, the direction was a straight shot on the *Départemental* 307 the whole way. I'd have to see the car at some point unless it had been impounded. Sure enough, about two miles from her work, there was Dwayne, hasard lights flashing out his uselessness. Luckily, the single lane was a bit wider in that stretch, so other cars could pass the van without crossing over the dividing line.

I climbed aboard Dwayne. It wasn't electrical, because the hazard lights were working. Looking at the instrument panel, about every other warning light was on as well. They were all red, the dash color of death. Turning the spare key, nothing happened- no sound, no reaction. Just as well, because the manual told me to interpret the signals as 'stop the motor immediately.' The Caravan would need to be towed.

I called our insurer to see if our policy might cover the tow. The insurance company would only send a tow truck if the car was more than 50 kilometers from home.

Dwayne was too close. I'd have to pay for it myself.

But tow him where? I didn't want to give any more money to the charlatans who'd fleeced me thousands just to swap out the lights. Besides, that dealership was at least 20 kilometers in the opposite direction. Then, I remembered there was a place that sold US Cars in Saint-Cloud. That was only about five kilometers away, and they hadn't yet screwed me. This would be their chance.

They'd need a day to diagnose Dwayne. So, I went home to contemplate my failing decision-making aptitude. I thought back to the parable a psychologist friend of mine related about manholes. A patient was walking down the sidewalk when they stepped unexpectedly into an open manhole cover. They fell hard and awkwardly, twisting as they tumbled and breaking several bones badly. The shock was profound, and it took them a long time to climb out of the hole and treat their wounds.

A while after they recovered, they were walking down a different sidewalk when they noticed another manhole uncovered in front of them. "Hey, I recognize that," they say to themself, "that's a manhole without a cover on it. If I keep going, I'll fall down and hurt myself." At which point, they step in and do just that. It's what they know. It's familiar, like an abusive relationship.

Eventually, the patient works up the courage to avoid the manholes, breaking the pattern. My personal waypoint was at more than a dozen manholes in my trouble with roads and cars in France. When would I finally flip the turn signal?

"We found out what was wrong with your Caravan," said the voice on the phone. That sounded promising.

"The blah blah on the engine was under stress by the weakness of the blah, resulting in loss of oil and then failure." I *had* noticed lately that we needed to keep putting in a liter of oil every week or so. "Did the car experience any shock to the undercarriage recently?"

"If you mean like an accident or going over rocks or something like that, no. However, there are an incredible amount of speed bumps in our area."

"That could have caused the crack."

"So, can you repair, or replace the broken part?"

"The broken part is the motor. You'll have to replace the whole engine."

I was incredulous. This couldn't be! Had our entire investment just gone up in smoke? A complete loss? I thought, even bankruptcy creditors got 10 cents on the dollar.

I regained a modicum of composure and asked how much engine replacement would cost. He explained that it was more than the car was worth. I wailed that I didn't know what to do, but I wanted to ask for a second opinion. Thankfully, he refrained from telling me I was also ugly.

The mechanic used his most compassionate voice to tell me that I'd better decide quickly, because he wanted the hunk of junk off his lot ASAP, and he'll charge me €50 per day parking for every day past Friday. Oh, and don't forget I owe him €100 for the DOA diagnosis.

It was useless. Other garages told me that if there was a crack in the engine block, it was toast. The motor only had 71 000 miles on it. Did my insurance cover this, perchance? No way. How about them helping me go after the city for installing all the donkey backs that broke my machine? Nope, and anyway I couldn't prove that the speed bumps were 100% responsible for the car's demise. There was only one thing to do- call the undertaker.

The junk man was happy to tow away the car for free, if I gave it to him outright, new tires and all. We scheduled a pickup time and I showed up early to say my goodbyes. I cleared out the CDs, squeegee, shopping bags and other crap we had accumulated. There were maps of faraway places we'd visited, and brochures of campsites the car had taken us to. I gathered the remaining sticks of gum, loose change and toys for a much younger boy.

Dwayne had been legit in France for a total of six months before undergoing euthanasia. He donated his organs and we didn't get anything for their resale.

CHAPTER TWENTY-EIGHT

Borne 675 - Citroën Neveragain

Citroën Plusjamais

With Dwayne deceased, the Fiat was our only car left. It was a good backup or second car, but too tiny to satisfy our daily needs. So, we went shopping for a primary vehicle, another minivan like our recently departed.

What we think of as a minivan in the 'States is considered humongous over here. Flintstone brontasaurus big. There's nothing 'mini' about an American minivan. So, it takes some adjustment when you ask to see a minivan in France, and the dealership shows you something which would fit in the back seat of an American minivan.

We wouldn't be fooled this time with one of those

strange foreign makes. We'd learned our lesson and were set on a French-built *bagnole*, with the associated network of repair centers, and local reputation for a decent resale value. This meant choosing among Renault, Peugeot and Citroën.

Of the three, Citroën has a history of being the most innovative in terms of design. Not innovative in the terms of being the first to create something that others then copy. No. Citroën creates designs that NOBODY copies.

One of those was the body of the DS in the 1950s. A Citroën designer must have seen a sleek sports car, with a low front bumper, and lines slowly rising to the inclined windshield, and said to himself "Wow, that looks aerodynamic and sporty! What if we turned the body around and made it drive backwards?" Thus the DS was born, a right triangle with the fat part facing forward. The front wheels of the DS were wider apart than the back wheels. When the writers of the Mentalist series wanted to give the main character, Patrick Jane, a quirky car to go with his ascerbic and intellectual personality, they appropriately chose the DS.

Before the DS, Citroën's claim to fame was the 2 CV, also known as the '*deux chevaux*' or 'two horsepower.' That's what the French affectionately call it. English nicknames include the "Flying Dustbin" or "Tin Snail." Mass-produced at practically the same time as the Volkswagen Beetle, the 2 CV had the same intent: an inexpensive, reliable, high gas mileage utility vehicle which could handle the rough terrain of post-war Europe. Whereas the Beetle sold 21 million units in its first 40-odd years, the 2CV sold nearly three times less. Why? Well, one reason is that the original model had a top speed of 40 mph.

Another is that it was kooky with quirks. Instead of having the driver's side window roll down, it folded up. The back passenger windows didn't open at all. The windshield wipers only worked when the car was in motion. To wash the windscreen, you squashed a rubber bulb on the floor with your foot. The body of the 2CV was paper thin. The steering wheel was 'Q-shaped,' with one spoke attaching to the column on a single point on the wheel. This left 350° of the wheel floating in the air, unstable and shaking at the slightest bump. These aspects made the 2 CV distinctive, but not big sellers in Europe outside France, and practically unheard of in the biggest auto market in the world, the USA.

The modern model of Citroën which caught our eye was what they call here a '*monospace*.' It wasn't any bigger than a regular car, just taller. You couldn't fit any more people, or groceries, or appliances. However passengers could wear a stove-pipe hat comfortably. The model was pretentiously named the Picasso. Don't think about the artist's 'blue' period. Think 'cubism,' when the artist put an eye where the nose goes, and the ear where the mouth goes. That's what Citroën decided to do with the car's interior parts.

One of the design anomalies they chose was to put the stick-shift on the dashboard. Was there some flaw in the floorboard stickshift? No. Was there some advantage to having the stick on the dash? No. It was simply, "We're Citroën, and we do things differently, so there." Every time we wanted to eject a CD, we needed to downshift.

Also, all of the indicators, like speed, fuel, etc. were in the center of the dash, set well back. You needed to constantly turn your head to the right to see how fast you were going. And because the numbers were digital only, no needles, whenever the sun was overhead or behind, you couldn't read anything.

It was too modern for its own good. "Why use mechanical solutions, when we can deploy buttons, glorious buttons!" We subsequently learned to our dismay that this total reliance on electronics was to be the car's downfall.

The parking brake and starter were engaged by pressing round plastic! That means when the battery dies, there's no way to save yourself by getting the car moving and popping the clutch! Believe me, I tried.

Once when I stupidly left the lights on all night, it wouldn't start. Parked on an incline, I had the brilliant idea of a good ol' revival with rollin' and poppin'. After about 50 presses on the parking brake button, the car unblocked itself and allowed me to roll forward. Haha! I've out-smarted the technology! I steered into the center of the one-way, one-lane residential street. As parked cars whizzed by faster, I felt my David vs. Goliath moment was near. I popped that mutha.

Suddenly everything came alive! There was a loud buzzing, red indicators filled the dash and all four wheels locked simultaneously. My foot was on the gas but I wasn't going anywhere. It ended as soon as it began. The lights and sounds faded as a last gasp from the 0.0001% charged battery. Now the car blocked the road, immobile and shoulder-to-shoulder with other parked cars. Neighbors were soon to appear in my rear-view mirror, none too pleased about being unable to go neither forward nor back.

I resolved to abandon playing MacGyver. All I wanted now was to park the thing out of the way. I pressed the parking break button maybe 100 more times before the Picasso released me from its clutches and let me come to rest on a curb. I had escaped, and took the train to work to walk off my brush with a superior life form. Later that week, I got a jump which offered just enough juice to drive her to a dealer service station.

We should have known better. Citroën is just one letter removed from the French word '*citron*,' which means 'lemon' in English.

As is my bent, I rechristened the car the Citroën Neveragain. I vowed never to purchase another.

CHAPTER TWENTY-NINE

Borne 700 - Driving school on strike

Auto-école en grève

One day I showed up, and the front door of my *auto-école* was locked. There was a note on the door, indicating a *'grève,'* meaning they were on strike. I was puzzled, because I knew the business to be a sole proprietorship. She couldn't have been protesting the working conditions, or wages set by the boss, because she *was* the boss.

I shouldn't have been surprised. In France, everybody goes on strike. It's not just blue-collar workers. It's not just people in unions, like teachers, nurses, flight attendants and bus drivers. Firemen go on strike. Policemen go on strike. Dentists go on strike. Doctors go on strike. Judges go on strike.

It's as if the 1789 Revolution never ended. In fact, reform happens quite often in France, and the great majority of people benefit. However, acceptance never comes without massive noise and vitriol and protest marches. The Revolution provided a blueprint for change that's still widely revered, apart the rolling of heads.

I went back home and did some independent study with my student guide book. Chapter one on signals was by far the longest chapter, at 60 pages. In chapter one I learned there were 600 different kinds of road signs in France. Can you imagine? Most signs have pictograms which must be memorized. There are separate road signs warning of wild animals, and domesticated animals. Separate road signs indicating alpine skiing and nordic skiing. Separate signs for 'warning: bump' and 'warning: two bumps.' There's one forbidding access to wooden pushcarts.

There are at least five separate signs forbidding bicycles, scooters, motorcycles, all motorized vehicles, and all motorized vehicles with the exception of scooters. There are an additional five signs obligating these different options of locomotion to use a certain road, and not any other. Both forbidding and requiring use the same symbol, so you need to be able to tell them apart by their color or shape. Signs are so specific, that you sometimes run across 10 or more of them bunched up on the same set of poles. You need to be a speed reader to ingest all of them.

Often signs are completed by other smaller signs, specifying something about the first sign. 'YOU CAN'T DRIVE HERE,' it'll shout, followed by a little whisper, 'if you're a three-ton truck.' You slam on the brakes until you're right on top of it and realize it doesn't apply to you. Even if you're in a three-ton truck it can be confusing. One sign forbids access if you have two tons over the same axel. Do delivery drivers really calculate the weight on their front tires separately from their back tires? If a truck drove over a stone bridge and it collapsed, would engineers come and weigh front and back separately to determine if a law was broken?

One of the signs I had a hard time getting used to was the white circle with the black diagonal line through it. In the US, that means 'forbidden' like 'Don't smoke' or 'Do not enter.' In France, it just means, 'you know that thing we told you about earlier, well, now it doesn't apply any more.' Crossing the sign, you have to harken back to what signs you just passed. You'll see a line through a bicycle, for example, meaning the end of a bike lane. Bikes are still allowed, they just don't have their own lane anymore.

For parking, I was used to paid and free. Over here they have a couple more *quatre figures*, or alternatives for free parking. One is where the sign instructs you to put a cardboard disk on your dash, indicating when you arrived. The meter maids use that to determine if you've overstayed your welcome. Here's a money-making idea I'll give you for free. You know those stupid birthday cards which play a song, or activate a moving character when you open them? They prove that you can put a little battery or motor in between sheets of paper undetected. Will somebody please work with a Chinese manufacturer to make my French village disk turn automatically so I can park near the train station all day?

Some French neighborhood streets are just wide

enough to accomodate parked cars on one side or the other. Rather than create jealousy between the folks on the even side and the odd side, the signs instruct parkers to use *stationnement alterné* or to alternate sides. The 1st through the 15th of the month, they're all on one side, the 16th through the end of the month, they're all on the other side. That's the theory anyway. What happens is that on the 1st and the 16th, cars are parked on *both* sides. Drivers try to slalom in-between the legal and illegal parked cars. Sometimes, the street will simply be at a standstill for several minutes. Stressed commuters yell at each other, one tries to direct traffic, another goes up on the curb and around. It's great entertainment if you're not behind a windshield.

Once, at the beginning of the month, when it seemed the whole neighborhood was on vacation but me, I arrived on my block when there were no other parked cars. It was then that I realized that the sign didn't indicate which side was 1-15 and which side was 16-31. I idled while I tried to remember where the car was parked when I grabbed it that morning. I didn't recall, so I flipped a coin. I came out later that day to find several other cars had joined mine in the same line. I had guessed correctly! Looking closer, I noticed we all had parking tickets. Pity the fools who thought I knew what I was doing.

Upon returning to the *auto-école* the week following the '*grève*' notice, I asked the young lady behind the desk what the strike was all about. "Oh, we're protesting that it takes too long for the *Préfecture* to give students an appointment to pass the written test."

"But won't your strike delay the process even

further? When your office is closed, students can't prepare. Isn't that counter-productive?"

"Not if the government listens to us. Last weekend we were thousands of *auto-écoles* on strike all over France."

"Isn't this, like, the third time you've gone on strike for this same issue? Have you noticed any change?"

A grumpy face.

"That reminds me of something else that's strange," I said. "I've been registered here for two years, and you've never presented me to pass the real test."

She coughed. "Well, as you know, there were some administrative hold ups with your file at the *Préfecture*. They're always asking for something new and always so slow to respond..."

"Yes, but you've sent other students of your school to the *Préfecture* for the real test."

"Effectively, that is correct, but, of course, they've been passing tests here for a certain time, and, in a consistent manner, getting 35 or better."

"OK," I said. "That sounds reasonable." And then I slinked into the classroom and got a 25. I said to myself, "this might take many more years."

CHAPTER THIRTY

Borne 725 - Deer Madame Start

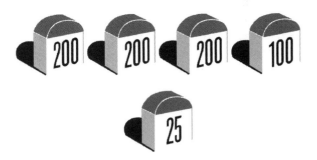

Deer Madame Start

May is confirmation season in France. Pre-teen boys and girls across the land go hunting for *cadeaux*. After all, something must sustain them through the long months of Catholic inquisitioning. Certainly the ceremony is not their reward. Standing solemnly in their hotel bathrobe, offering an oversized white phallus on fire to a droning lecturer... surely this is not their idea of a Sunday well-spent? No, after the sacrifice, their must be gifts. And the Starts wouldn't miss it for the world.

"Cherie, couldn't we just send money?"

"No, we must BE there, IN PERSON."

"But with Paul's Saturday afternoon double-header, we won't be able to leave until late at night. We'll get no sleep on the 6-hour drive, and have to hop right back in the car after the meal to make it home late Sunday night. A school night. A work night."

"*Pas question!* We will go."

"OK, but I'll let *you* drive through the night. I'm sleeping in the back."

Our negotiations concluded and I setup a makeshift bed in the Citroën Neveragain. I folded down the back seat and placed a single air mattress over both it and a suitcase. It was far from level, but at least the 20% incline had my head above my feet, which pushed against the hatchback. Junior was riding shotgun, with his seat reclined as far back as it could go. My wife took the controls and we set off over desolate village streets into the black night.

You know how the traffic school books say that most accidents happen less than a mile from home? Well, they're right!

Elongated on my back, I watched the moon moving through the trees of a wood that we crossed on our way. As my mind drifted off to the prelude of those dreamy dreams, I was abruptly hurtled toward the front seat. The driver's headrest halted me by twisting my neck and shoulders. Through three-way shouting, I turned and looked through the windshield and saw nothing. We were at a dead stop. Not another car was on the road. Aurore started crying.

"What's wrong? Why did you slam on the brakes?"

"Oh, I hurt her!"

"Her?!?! What about me?!?! The stop nearly broke my neck!"

"She came out of nowhere, from the right side."

"Who did? A pedestrian? I don't see anyone."

"No," sobbing harder, "une *biche*!"

"A bitch?"

"It's a deer, Dad," my son chimed in.

"Oh, a deer, a female deer," I sang. "But I didn't feel a collision. Or hear one, for that matter. Are you sure you hit the deer?"

"Yes! It's horrible! She ran off that way. We must find her!"

"Find her? What for?"

"Whu-huh, whu- when you kill a deer," sniff "you must take it to the school" hiccup "so they can feed the students."

"Huh? That's the most ridiculous..."

"It's the *law*!" My wife was adamant. "Otherwise, hunters would kill out of season, and keep the meat for themselves."

"Maybe in the countryside, but I can't imagine that happens here. No Parisian cop's gonna ask you if you have a license to hunt deer with your car!"

My silly comments didn't stop her tears. "OK, let me take a look." I slid off the mattress and out the passenger door to inspect the right front bumper. I saw nothing at first in the darkness, but then noticed a small dent on the hood. The right wheel-well panel was a bit detached. I re-clipped it and remarked that it had also bent. There was no blood and no body.

197

"Listen, the deer ran off, so she must be all right. There's no sign it's hurt."

"Really?" Somewhat reassured, my wife blew her nose and I got back in. She set off slowly, turning the headlights into the woods. We saw no signs of wildlife, nor wild death.

The rest of the drive and the weekend went off without further a-doe. In the light of the day, the damage to the Citroën Neveragain was superficial. The only minor annoyance was that the parking guidance sensors no longer functioned.

We phoned up our insurance company and explained the situation. They weren't going to reimburse us so easily.

"Since there were no witnesses, no police and no accident report, you must produce other evidence proving that it was really a collision with a deer."

"Like what?"

"You must submit samples of fur collected from the spot of impact." Aurore hung up, stunned, and repeated the request.

"Who are we, CSI?" I said. "What are they going to do with the fur? DNA test the beast for suicidal genes?"

The bumper and grill didn't retain any fur, or it had long since blown away on the 1 000 kilometer round-trip.

"Who cares?" I dismissed. "Let's just give them cat hair! At least that stupid Timinou would serve a purpose in our family. They're not going to have a veterinarian forensics expert investigate the accident for cryin' out loud!"

"No, but cat hair is obviously not deer fur. It must come from a wild animal." We looked around the house. There was no real fur on any of our clothes. We did live for

10 years in the People's Republic of Berkeley, after all.

I did find a set of tongs for cutting meat which had a very classy hoof for a handle. An outdoorsy relative must have given it to us as a present. I couldn't tell if it was from a deer or a goat or a wild boar. No matter, its fur was rejected by Madame as too old, too dead and probably treated with too many chemicals to be believed.

She called her family. Her father and brother-in-law and nephew all hunted from time-to-time. Maybe they'd contribute a carcass to our car case? After some convincing that, no, we really didn't want something useful like a leg from their most recent kill, they agreed to shear and send. A day later, in an envelope, we got the real McCoy. We brought the fur, along with the car, down to the dealership repair shop to be inspected by an assigned accident 'expert' from the insurance company.

"OK, we agree it was a deer." Success! "Although we can't be completely sure of the driver's intent, nor if the accident could have been avoided. That's why we gladly offer to pay half the damages."

"Half?!" I questioned the deer hunter, when she relayed the verdict. "Do they expect us to go after the uninsured animal for the rest?"

CHAPTER THIRTY-ONE

Borne 750 - Company car

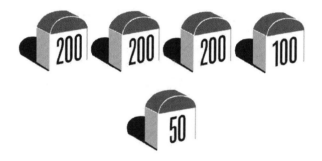

Voiture de fonction

After six years in France, I switched to a different company. Part of my new compensation package was a company car. How could they give a company car to someone without a French driver's license? Who knows? This wasn't part of the checking procedure.

It's fairly common in France to be offered the use of a car for customer-facing jobs. Nearly 90% of French companies give a company car to at least one of their employees. There's a total of five million company cars. One out of every three cars sold in France is to a company or government administration.

The car could take the form of a *'véhicule de service'* or a *'voiture de fonction.'* A service vehicle is like the Post Office jeep. Many workers use the same car, and nobody can drive it for their personal use.

A *'voiture de fonction'* is mainly to be used for a worker's trips to see clients, or to get to and from work from home. It's part of his compensation, and thus an integral part of the employment contract.

The value of a company car is typically commensurate with the worker's hierarchical status in the organization. Variations can be negotiated if the car aspect is less or more important to a certain worker. It's a lot easier to negotiate up for a newer model, or fancier features, than to convince the employer to grant a higher base salary or bonus. This is because most organizations who offer company cars have a sizeable lot of cars to choose from, and a relationship with a dealer specializing in fleet management for corporations. The dealer has access to many more cars in other fleets that they can easily swap out to meet a particular need.

I preferred a larger car, because I had a family. The size wasn't a problem for parking because I lived in the 'burbs. The company was happy to oblige because someone with a station wagon had recently left the company. They explained that the departed employee had received it new three years ago, so I was happy with the prospect of having the use of a fairly modern car. I'd only ever had one new car in my life. Plus this was a German make, and I always preferred the handling of *Fahrvergnügen*. They loaned me a Volkswagen Passat.

I was all excited walking down to the parking garage to see my new car. The HR lady didn't know where it was exactly. It had sat there for a couple months, since the previous employee had left. I walked from level -1 round and round down to level -4 pressing the key button and looking for a flash of recognition. People I passed must have thought I was an idiot who didn't remember where he parked his car.

Finally, at level -5, a vague yellow light cut through the dust. I approached and saw a car that was not like the others. It was parked in-between two other black cars, but mine was gray from all the accumulated filth. It had tire sized dents on both sides, and scratches everywhere. Many were likely intentional, as the previous driver had parked somewhat sideways, annoying anyone who might take the slot on either side. Inside there were other parts broken, and the rear-view mirror lay uselessly on the passenger's seat. The floor was littered with used kleenex and half-eaten biscuits. It did start up, though. She sure was ugly, but she was all mine.

The HR department explained that the car could be used as I wished: for work, for errands, on weekends. Could I loan it to a co-worker? Yes. Could I loan it to my wife? Yes. It was part of my compensation, and thus, I could do as I pleased with the 'money' I earned.

I knew I'd take the train almost exclusively, since the commute was only a half an hour on one direct line. That left the Passat to be driven by Aurore. To and from work. To pick up our son. To the grocery store. Anywhere. I only used it on the weekends, or to get to the airport for business trips. Together, we took that car all over Europe: Spain, the Netherlands, Brittany, the United Kingdom, even Ireland by ferry.

The company would pay for the parking spot near the offices. This was a big deal, because parking was scarce and expensive in La Défense, the crowded business center to the west of Paris. Here, France's only skyscrapers reigned. They were filled daily with 180 000 workers. In addition, the company would pay for the insurance, the fuel, and wear and tear such as replacing the tires.

The only things I'd have to pay for myself would be upkeep like washing, tolls, insurance premiums for damage and, of course, traffic tickets. How would that work, since the owner or lessee is the company, not the driver? Well, the company has a list of which car is assigned to which employee, and when they receive a ticket notification, they pass it along to that employee.

Sounds simple enough, but I learned that in practice, there's a vast black market for passing the buck. Co-workers often exchanged each others' cars. Whoever got a ticket could either pay it and have his points deducted, or find another person with more points to give, and have that person take the fall. The original offender would pay the fine, but he'd also have to pay some other kind of compensation to the fall guy. It could be as simple as offering dinner, or a bottle of champagne, but could run into helping move for the weekend, or painting a room. Since these were mostly sales people, leads and accounts could also be transacted.

Fortunately, I never needed to find a fall guy. My failsafe was the ineptitude of the system. I didn't trade my perfect record to bail out my colleagues, mostly because my status was a bit precarious. Although I wouldn't get pinged for the occasional PV (*proces verbal*), it might draw unwanted attention if suddenly dozens of infractions were attributed to my name.

So, my wife did the driving, I got the tickets, no points were lost, and we both were perfect law-abiding specimens as far as the administration was concerned.

In fact, around this time, the *Préfecture* sent my wife a special communication. When an envelope arrives from the *Préfecture*, you expect the worst. "What did I do this time?" you ask yourself. Inside she found the following letter:

"*Monsieur le Préfet* and his staff would like to acknowledge that during the past five years, we have not constated any road violations emanating from your permit. We would like to congratulate you for your perfect driving record."

Of course, madame *had* been at the wheel of most of our radar-recognized violations, because she used the car more than me. She just hadn't been credited with any tickets. She got a lot of mileage out of showing that letter to astonished friends and family. To this day, we've never met another person who received a similar commendation, whether deserving or unwarranted. Praise from the authorities in France is extremely rare.

We could now get rid of the Fiat. The Accompli had accomplished all it was gonna, and could now be put out to pasture. It had 173 000 kilometers on it from two owners in 17 years, which was rather mild usage. However, that was made up for by an extraordinary ability to create condensation on the interior windows in virtually all weather conditions. That, and the glove box, which was held in by a wine cork, would randomly open, knocking the unsuspecting passenger hard on the kneecaps. I was floored when someone offered nearly the same price we had paid for it six years hence. Of the 10 cars I've owned in my life, it's the only one I didn't lose money on - *fait accompli*!

CHAPTER THIRTY-TWO

Borne 775 - Maximilien

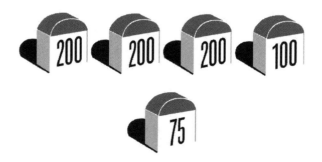

Maximilien

"Hello granny, it's Max, *ça va?* Yes, I'm well. Clara, too, she's also doing good. I'm not bothering you?

You were watching who? Zorro? Oh, Navarro, the inspector. You've seen the episode before. Ah-huh, it was the corrupt mayor who did it, I see. So, we can speak now, then?

Yes, I still have the same job. In Paris, yes, actually

La Défense anyway, in the outskirts. The business center, what.

To cut to the chase, I'm calling you from the office for something work-related. Yes, I'm working right now. We're in open space, everyone can hear me, so I'll try to be quick. It's not too loud for you? No? OK, I'll continue, then.

I have a favor to ask you. *Comment?* No, I don't need money, but that's kind of you, grandma. Yes, I'm doing fine financially, well, with buying the apartment we've had to tighten our belts a bit, but I can't complain. What's that? Yes, still in telecom, er, related to telecommunications, it's video conferencing for enterprise, I mean, businesses, big businesses y'know. Do you know Skype? No? On your computer. You don't have a computer? I'll show you on my computer someday. Then, you'll understand better. Right.

Anyway, I wanted to ask you to help me with my car. No, I wasn't in an accident, knock on wood. Um-hm that *would* be bad, an accident. Like who? Uncle Théophile was in an accident? Is he OK? Oh, I thought you meant recently. No, I guess they didn't have airbags back in the '70s.

Yes, I drive safely, well, er fast, but I can handle it- and it's really for that- the purpose of my call. I got a ticket.

No, not a chicken, a *ti-cket*, for speeding. No, I wasn't pulled over. I was flashed, from behind. No, behind the car, the back of the... the rear license plate. They didn't get my photo. Just the car's. And that's why I'm able to ask you for a favor.

It's a company car, so anyone can drive it. Yes, even my girlfriend or someone I loan it to. That's permitted. For that reason, I'd like to say that it was you behind the wheel.

Yes, I know it wasn't you. No, you've never driven

my car. But the authorities, they don't know that. They have no idea. It's just that they'll take another two points away from me for going 25 kilometers per hour over. I only have a couple points left. How many? Maybe six, maybe four, maybe two, how the hell do I know? So it's risky for me. To lose points.

Excuse me? No, 25 kilometers over is nothing on the *Autoroute*. It's just coasting. Hell, my last trip in Germany, I did 180 easy, and nobody bothered me. The Krauts all drive that fast. No, of course not, I don't drive 180 in France. This time they got me at 155. And if I only have two points left, all it takes is one false move, and I have to start from scratch to get my license again.

Do you know what that means? Paying a driving school, taking both tests, or waiting ages to get to take it. Only an idiot would go back and do that again. And meanwhile, I won't be able to drive at all. I'll be fu... er, um, I'll be in a bad way.

But not you, right? You have all your points, *non*? You don't know. Well, have you gotten any tickets lately? How about last month? The last three years? *Voilà*, you have all 12 points, then. So, two little points off won't do you any harm. But for me, it would be *la cata*, a real catastrophe.

My co-workers? They're like me. They pick up tickets right and left, and try to pin them on someone else. And Uncle Charles, he already helped me out like this. And my *cousine*, Emilie, did too. She's studying in Québec, so she doesn't care. The points she takes for me will disappear when she comes back from university in four years. But she's already helped me out twice, so…

Of course, of course I'll pay for it! You don't have to pay for anything. I'll take care of every single thing from my end. Ah, *mémé*, you've saved me. You're an angel. You're a pearl. Really! Truthfully. No, but I must say it, because it's true.

There's a way I could repay you? Sunday? Oh yeah? You still do the traditional Sunday lunch, do you? *Every* Sunday? I think I've got something going on with my girlfriend, but... Rabbit in a mustard sauce? A cake also? Isn't that a bit much? Is it a special occasion? No, of course I like it, but Clara is a vegetarian, you know. And La Creuse is six hours, round trip.

Oh, it's very nice of you to invite us to stay Saturday night. There's a what? A *guinguette*? Oh, dancing in the festival hall. The *accordéon* isn't really my thing. I'm more into electro. Tecktonik. It's a dance. Maybe some other time.

In any case, a thousand thanks for your help with the points. Big kisses. I'll tell her. Hugs to *pépé* also. Big kisses. Salut."

CHAPTER THIRTY-THREE

Borne 800 - Pitching for Pentecost

Lancer pour le Pentecôte

We're on the freeway at 5 p.m., heading west in bumper-to-bumper. It's a three-day weekend, and the weather is predicted to be hot in Brittany. Half of Paris it seems is driving in the same direction as the Sun.

We get Monday off for Pentecost. What is Pentecost? I didn't know when I arrived. It was just a cool word with staccato rhythm in a Paul Simon song. I came to learn it's another holiday that the old Catholics usurped, this time from Jewish tradition. From what I understand, 40 days after the resurrection, the 'spirit' of God descended on the apostles. This was so important way back when that the

Sunday religious *fête* needed to be extended to a Monday holiday, the *'Lundi de Pentecôte.'* It stuck, even though less than 1% of the modern population observes anything on the Pentecost. It should be called 'I don't give a Whit Sunday.'

The government tried to capitalize on this *blasé* sentiment, transforming the *Lundi de Pentecôte* into the *'journée de solidarité.'* The holiday became just another working day, however the earnings would be given to a fund for the aged or infirm. Well, you can't take something from a worker in France without giving him something in return. So, after a year of the Solidarity Day, and fervent negotiations from unions, some employers decided to just give the day off anyway. Some people work, and others don't. The employers who gift the Day often wait until the last minute to inform workers, so they can't plan. It's chaos and uncertainty as usual. I took a personal day off to be sure, not worrying if I could have had it for free. I'm used to two weeks a year in the 'States, so I don't complain about losing one measly day out of a month of vacation days.

You'd think that *this* Pentecost folks might sit out the three-day weekend, or depart on Saturday morning instead. After all, workers have already had three long weekends this very month. We've been spoiled. Every year in May, the 1st, the 8th and Ascension (another catholic holdover) are national holidays. Ascension is always on a Thursday, so always a day off from work. Most people *'font le pont,'* by taking Friday off and bridging Ascension into a four-day weekend. This year, 2009, the 1st and 8th also came on Mondays (the day off is lost if they fall on a weekend). With Pentecost falling in the same month, that makes this one of those Magic months of May, with a whopping four long weekends.

That's in addition to the three-day weekend in April for Easter. Yep, that's another one, which extends to a holiday on Monday. It's not on Sunday that the bunny delivers chocolates. It's on Monday that the church bell hides Haribo.

Personally, I'd prefer to avoid the traffic, but this weekend I'm committed. There's a baseball tournament.

I know what you're thinking, "Baseball in France?" It's true, there are more players signed up for leagues playing *pétanque*. Three dozen times more. However, there are enough youth baseball teams in the Paris region to play a whole six-month season without facing the same opponent more than twice. You just sometimes have to drive two hours to get to the field.

Now, I use the term 'baseball' loosely in the French Little League. Many coaches adopt the loud, aggressive soccer-style approach, and push their players to run, run, run. On a grounder to the second baseman, the first-base coach windmills his arm, cajoling his 9-year-old to round the base and keep going. They don't care if the infielder has the ball in their glove standing right in the base path, they still tell the runner to go. What should be an insane risk at any playing level unfortunately pays off for the unsportsmanlike coach if the force play at first is missed. The inexperienced defense throws around the horn backwards, chasing the runner until the ball arrives at the catcher just after an inside-the-infield home run. These runs are celebrated by the opposition with the same fervor as if something remarkable has just been accomplished.

On board the bus, there are about 30 kids, 10 adults and one bus driver. She came in the package deal with the bus company. The arrangement is that she drives us there on Friday, we put her up in a hotel for three nights and pay for all her meals, and she drives us back on Monday. Four hours there. Four hours back. For the equivalent of 1 days' work, she gets 2 1/2 days' vacation, all expenses paid. Sweet deal.

In this traffic it'll take longer than four hours. No worries, I'm not driving. I can converse and play cards. It reminds me of trips to camp as a kid. I sing a few bars of 'Another One Rides the Bus.' No takers. '99 bottles of beer on the wall?' That gets them going. After a while, I regret my suggestion. Unbelievably, two kids sing all the way from 99 down to zero, including my own. That's my boy!

After two hours, we pull off to a rest stop and picnic area. Did someone ask her to stop? It's not to let us go to the bathroom- there's a toilet on the bus. It's not for fuel-the tank is full and this stop doesn't have a gas station nor convenience store, nor restaurant. Besides, we brought sandwiches with us. We can't eat on the bus, so now's a good a time as any to have dinner.

The kids wolf down the meal in 15 minutes, and we're still standing around. Legs stretched? OK, let's get back on the road. Everybody climbs back aboard, except for one person. The bus driver doesn't move.

I'm the only adult who speaks French, so I'm prodded to go speak with her to find out what's going on.

"Hi, we're ready to go if you are." I give her a big smile.

"The pause isn't over yet, *monsieur*."

"Pause? What pause, *madame*?"

"For every two hours' driving time, I must take a break for 45 minutes."

This was beyond my comprehension. I remember driving from San Francisco to Los Angeles dozens of times with just one stop for gas. A couple of times I made it all the way to San Diego with a single stop. We weren't asking her to do anything close to that. This drive to Brittany was similar in distance to an L.A. to Las Vegas trip. Almost everyone does that in one fell swoop, evidenced by the lack of service stations along the way. There are many stretches of 30+ miles without gas.

"Who says you must do that? Is it a law or something?"

"No, the law is four hours thirty, but my company and our drivers have a higher standard for safety. Taking a pause every two hours, we stay alert."

You could say that again. At this rate, we'd be up all night on the road.

I explained our predicament to the rest of the crew. The messenger was shot full of holes.

"That's ridiculous!"

"Ludicrous!"

"Can't you negotiate with her?"

"It appears to be a part of her employment contract. One of those unbreakable rules, I guess."

"Who's to know? We won't tell anyone that she drove after 'only' a 15-minute break. Sheesh! Can't you convince her to get a move on?"

"I've been on the losing end of these things before. If I push too hard, she could refuse to continue."

"You mean go on strike right here? Right now?"

"She could leave us all stranded by the side of the road?"

"Yeah. I've heard stories..."

The frustration died down as we amused ourselves with thoughts of what we could have done. Plans went from breaking the bus clock, to tying her up in the hold as someone else took the wheel. She eventually climbed back aboard at the 45-minute mark to the sound of our laughter. Taking that as a sign of our approval of protocol, she drove off.

The traffic had not abated, and was still moving along at an *escargot's* pace. Now we were behind thousands more late leavers. Three full lanes stretched out before the windshield farther than the eye could see. Out the window, a TGV flashed past at 300 kilometers an hour.

We resumed games and jokes. The kids were still excited at this point. As the wheat fields billowed slowly by, time marched on. The sun began to set. Sure enough, at 9:45 p.m., the bus pulled off the road again.

Knowing that something unpleasant is coming doesn't mean you're any more relieved when it arrives. None of us were hungry. None of us needed a smoke break. Nobody left the bus but the driver. We watched her from the window. She sat on a picnic bench in the dim lamplight, doing a crossword puzzle. By the arch of her neck and the proximity of her nose to the page, it appeared this activity taxed her eyes a lot more than watching the road.

"How much farther?"

"When will we get there?"

One of us had one of those revolutionary at the time smartphones with geolocalization. He said we were still about 100 kilometers away, so an hour in normal time. The traffic was moving better now. We saw several busses blow past at near speed-limit rates.

We tried to imagine the scene at arrival. Unloading

gear and sleepwalking kids in a cow pasture in the dark. How many of us brought flashlights? Could we set them up to shine in four directions as we pitched our tents in star formation? Not really. There were about 20 total tents to setup. We'd have to do them two by two. Which kids should we get to bed first? We didn't have the schedules yet, but we knew the first games would start at 9 a.m. Would one of our teams be on the slate that early? How should we organize ourselves to be ready?

We arrived at La Guerche de Bretagne near midnight, but we needn't have worried. The immaculate fields were lit by bright floodlights. Dozens of local volunteers greeted us and helped unload. The driver took the bus away for her all expenses paid weekend.

There were already dozens of tents lining the outfield perimeter from the earlier arriving teams. Their players were tossing and running on the biggest diamond. Our kids were wide awake and wanted to join them, so tents were set hastily and half-up as they dashed off. The adults finished the job, and got the gear inside, out of the dew of the night. One of us returned with the schedule.

"My cadet team's up to bat at 10 a.m., not so bad. Minime 1 starts at 11, and Joe, your minime 2 team doesn't start until noon." My kids could sleep in. I was relieved. I shouldn't have been.

The field lights were turned off at 1 a.m. and the wild kids finally ceded into the arms of Morpheus. At 4 a.m. the first bird chirped 'good morning!' He was soon joined by a cacophony of his brethren. The dawn slowly rose until the Sun peeked above the horizon at 6 a.m. I gave up on getting back to sleep and poked my head out of the tent. The fields were surrounded on three sides by tall trees.

Each one of them must have housed hundreds of feathered fiends.

Two of my players had decided to sleep out in the open. They were the Japanese kids. Even though we couldn't communicate in any common language, they were always prepared and eager. They were going to get the most out of the experience, and I wasn't going to stand in their way. Coach Joe was going to let all the kids be this morning. The day would be long and exhausting.

It was unbelievably hot that weekend in La Guerche. Brittany is known for rain and cool weather. It's very similar in climate to Ireland, which is one reason the Celts settled here. The meteorological maps displayed on the 8 o'clock news perennially show the hexagon's nose as grey, and speckled with numbers in the teens and single digits. That Pentecost weekend the mercury was double the usual for Spring, every day over 90 degrees in Fahrenheit.

I wanted my guys to rest, and not practice before the games. They were too excited and couldn't help themselves. I'd get two to stop playing catch and sit in the shade. There would still be six others horsing around in all corners of that expansive complex.

My team only had eight players, the minimum required. My ninth had begged off just before departure. There would be no substitutions. Everyone would have to play every inning and keep their energy until the end. My goal was to have the guys start refreshed. I didn't even manage one single game with an intact crew.

In the first inning of game one, the opponent's batter knocked a ball to right field. Rounding toward second at full speed, he knocked over the first baseman, my son. He stretched back his arms to slow his fall, dislocating his throwing elbow. I had to stay with the team, while a kind volunteer drove Paul to a doctor.

The umpire let us finish with seven players, calling an automatic out every time the 8th spot came up to bat. We lost the game, but kept the rest of the players from getting hurt.

I quickly went to negotiate with the coach of team one, to borrow one of his 10 players. He offered two in exchange for my best Japanese pitcher, and I readily accepted. I wanted to ensure my guys played, instead of sitting on the bench in a forfeit.

That they did, many of whom in positions they'd never played before. There were strict rules on the number of throws per day, so everyone pitched. This wasn't to our advantage, and we lost game two. This put us in the 2nd round pool which had to play a third game that same day, at 5 p.m. I looked at my guys' sweat-soaked jerseys, dusty faces, and half-opened eyes. They'd need extra fortification.

I ordered two sport drinks for each player, and had them chug them in the shade. A smiling Japanese boy then joined us. Team 1 had finished playing for the day, and our guy had rejoined the team for his fourth game of the day. We staggered to the finish line, completing our third game without forfeiting. We headed to the showers.

I ran into another coach as he came back from getting cleaned up. He looked very sunburnt.

"Man, I'm beat. All this exposure's getting to me."

"Me, too. Maybe we could have chosen a more relaxed way to spend a 3-day weekend."

"Yeah, the bus driver's dining on crêpes and cider, taking bubble baths in her personal tub and binge-watching Canal+ from her comfy bed in an air-conditioned hotel room. Meanwhile, we're in tents packed shoulder-to-shoulder, kept up 'til midnight by hundreds of rowdy kids, woken at 4 a.m. by thousands of freakin' birds, showering a dozen at a time and being scorched 15 hours a day by the Sun. And *we're* paying *her*? Something's wrong here."

I grinned back, too tired for a laugh. Washing away the day's dust made me a new man again. Back at the tent, I was greeted by a familiar face. My son had his right arm in a sling. His left arm held an Otter Pop. Nothing broken, but he'd stay on the DL for the weekend. I sought out the volunteer to thank her. The organizers went out of their way to make everything run smoothly. They went whole hog. Actually, three whole hogs.

Three entire pigs were roasted to feed the hundreds of players, coaches and fans. We pigged out while watching the evening's entertainment. Two contestants at a time were invited out on the big diamond, one on either side of home plate. They had to bend at the waist, place their head on the handle of a bat standing upright, turn three times, then run down the baseline, toward first or third. The first to touch the base won. Pair after pair of dizzy runners set off sideways, sometimes actually reaching the base. None of the players needed any cajoling to hit the sack before midnight that night.

The rest of the weekend went off without a hitch. When the bus came to pick us up, we were relieved. I have no idea if the bus driver's two hours on, 45 minutes off rhythm continued on the way back. I was sawing logs.

CHAPTER THIRTY-FOUR

Borne 825 - Free man in Paris

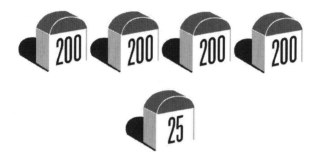

Candidat libre à Paris

By the Spring of 2010, I had had enough of my *auto-école*. They had never given me the chance to take the written test. This despite the fact that after six long years, I was still showing up Saturdays at their office. For the last two years I consistently got 35 or above on the mock tests.

This lack of attention was bad enough, but I was soon to be in real trouble. My California license was set to expire in a couple months. This time, the Department of Motor Vehicles wouldn't let me renew by mail. I had to go to the DMV in-person. I wasn't planning on going back to California until Christmas. I needed to hustle to meet regulations somewhere.

Luckily, a couple months later, in June, my company needed me in Phoenix for a meeting. Afterward, I took a couple days off, flying to Orange County. I surprised my Dad, seeing him on his birthday for the first time since moving to France seven years before.

We celebrated by making a father-son trip to the DMV! An eye exam, thumbprints, photo and $31 later, I had my California Driver's license renewed. The tense two-month limbo period was over. I could drive easy. I had at least one current valid license. A foreign one, that France still didn't recognize.

Back in France, I threatened to sue my *auto-école* unless they returned all my papers and gave me a full refund. I'm still waiting to get my money back.

I then sent my recovered documents to the powers that be, asking them to enroll me as a '*candidat libre*' or 'free' candidate to pass the written test. *Liberté.*

A month later the French administration asked me to submit an affidavit swearing that I was not signed up with an *auto-école*. Why this mattered, I have no idea. They must've thought, "We just want to make sure you're unprepared."

I *was* unprepared- for their *déjà vu* game of hot potato with the papers. A month after sending my sworn statement, they again asked for an affidavit that I was not signed up with an *auto-école*. Did the French hold

Groundhog Day in August?

I submitted the same letter a second time. Their response asked for the same thing, a third time. I was Bill Murray again. Then, I tried to play him in a different movie- Lost in Translation. My wife wrote the next missive, in Administrativese. I submitted her letter the third time, which was a charm. They accepted me as a free bird.

Now what? What else?- wait. And wait. Months passed without a word.

Every once in a while, for a laugh, I'd give them a call. "Who are you? Oh, no test date yet. Check back next month." Next Fall. Next Winter.

I had lots of time to do other things. Like reading. The light on the dash of the Citroën Neveragain read "Stop immediately, brakes defective." That sounded pretty serious, so we called the shop.

"It's probably nothing. Bring it in and we'll take a look at it."

"So you'll accept responsibility if the brakes go out on the way there?"

"I didn't say that. It's just that model has a tendency to go screwy with the wires."

He was right. There was nothing wrong with the brakes. The electrical system, however, was all messed up. It was giving false signals for problems that didn't exist. It was also indicating other things like 'add water to radiator' which were real. We couldn't tell which was which. The mechanic said it would be like that until we paid €811 to fix the electrical error. We bit the bullet.

A few days after bringing the car home, the same warning light came up again on the dash. WTF?

The shop told us that now it's indicating that the anti-lock braking system needs to be replaced, to the tune of €1 200. This, for a car which was only five years old. We weren't going to foot the bill alone. The mechanic himself admitted the car had design flaws. Doing our research in car magazines and internet user forums uncovered known issues. They'd sold us a lemon all right.

My wife used all her persuasion and patriotic fervor in a letter to the French automaker, saying she was happy to buy national, but if the manufacturer doesn't pick up the cost of repairing their obvious design flaws, we'd be in the *bleu, blanc, rouge*! She threatened to add our story to the countless others in the press about their crappy current. Citroën relented by offering a '*geste commercial*,' of only €500. They admitted no fault, and asked us to sign a paper acknowledging we were compensated for the issue, which really wasn't an issue as Citroën said, they were just being nice, no no no, not reimbursing, just helping, because they're a big-hearted company, not because they produce defective products. It was better than nothing, and we knew from experience how unlikely we were as consumers to get a better deal in this country. We took the lowball offer, reimbursing 1/4 of our expenses.

A year later we sold the car to friends. I don't want to call them ex-friends, but since the transaction, they don't drive by to see us much. Maybe their car won't let them.

CHAPTER THIRTY-FIVE

Borne 850 - Theoretical time

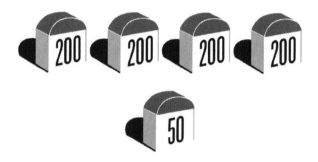

Examen théorique

My written test date was set for the following January, in Versailles. I drove past the glittering gates of the *château* of the Sun King. Acres and acres of his gardens blew past my window, and still the administration building was far from view. They really know how to make a fella feel small and insignificant.

I reached a row of 18th-century government

structures and parked. I entered the archway between numbers 22 and 26 and saw that number 24 was way in the back, down a long walkway. Boy did they have land to spare when they were constructing Versailles back in the day. The contrast from La Défense is like going from Manhattan to D.C.

The testing room was a grand auditorium. There must've been a hundred desks in there, and it wasn't even a quarter full. The chairs were set at least a body length apart from each other. All were facing a huge screen as if we were cars pulled up to the drive-in about to play the drag race scene from Rebel Without A Cause.

Each candidate gave their summons and ID to the front desk. In exchange, they were handed a gameboy. Well, that's what it looked like. Actually, a much older version, with only six buttons: A, B, C, D, Enter and Cancel. It reminded me of the handheld Coleco Electronic Football game I had as a kid. This should be a cinch!

We'd have 30 seconds to respond for each question. If we messed up, we could hit Cancel once and change the letters. We must hit Enter before the next question appeared, or our answer would not be recorded. It would be counted as wrong.

The exam began as the first image was shown on the screen, a street scene accompanied by a one-part multiple-choice question. The text was read aloud by a voice-over. Why did we need audio? Were there blind people taking the driving test? Then it was completely silent except for the click-clicking on our gameboys.

I knew the answer to the first one and responded quickly. And waited for the next one. There was no advantage to this. In a timed written test, you could answer the easy ones rapidly, and come back to the hard ones. You could deploy a strategy. Not here. The tricky ones and the two-part ones would have to be dealt with by fast thinking. And not listening.

Now, I have the kind of brain which is more sensitive to sound than images. I don't have a photographic memory, but I do have something akin to a musical memory. A crappy song will come out of the radio, crawl through my ear, and embed itself deep in my brain. There it will stay. It plants a flag, sets up a tent and invites fellow campers to join in a chorus of 'Hey, Soul Sister' by Train. You don't need the internet to RickRoll me. Just whisper 'never gonna give you up...' and walk away. That's all it takes.

The offending audio in my head cannot be blocked out. It must be replaced. Any song will do. Even another annoying song is preferable to what's been in my head for awhile. There's a big, big difference between five minutes of Lady Gaga, and 25 minutes.

The same thing happens to me with spoken text. I can't put it out of my mind, and instead concentrate on what I'm seeing. You know those laws that say you can't talk on the phone while driving? They're aimed at people like me. That's one law that I respect, even with a hands-free system.

Back to me in the exam auditorium. I'm trying to read the question quickly. But the voiceover is soooo muuuch slooower. Audio lady reads the text in about 25 seconds. If a candidate waited until she finished blabbing, he'd miss every answer for lack of response time.

So, I began humming. Very low. Just to myself. Enough to compete in my head with the voiceover vixen.

This worked for a handful of questions. Then I started to get looks. I'd have to develop a different strategy.

I placed the clicker on the desk and cupped my hands over my ears. I repeated my chosen letters in my head, then brought my hands down to quickly record them on the device before madame took over my cranium. The rest of the test was completed like this. I didn't care that my fellow candidates thought I was strange. I got through it, and that was the most important thing. Pride be damned.

We returned our gameboys and left. Nobody was told what score they got. The *auto-école* kids would hear from their school. The free candidates would get a letter at their home.

A week later mine came. They don't tell you which score you earned. Just pass or fail. I don't know if it was with flying colors or by the skin of my nose, but... I passed.

After seven long years of memorizing arcane vocabulary, complex math formulas and fighting the paperwork shuffle, I succeeded in passing that god-awful exam! In a language that was not my own.

However, I was only halfway there. Would it take *another* seven years to get that ridiculous pink paper?

CHAPTER THIRTY-SIX

Borne 875 - Prep for Practical

Preparation avant l'examen pratique

Three weeks later, I still hadn't heard about next steps. So, I wrote the DDEA. They're a curious hybrid organization overseeing 'equipment' and 'agriculture.' Maybe they're a relic from when farm boys moved up from tractors to automobiles.

They responded that if I still wanted to pursue the driving portion of the test as an independent candidate, that I needed to make a formal request. What? I had to ask again? Did they really think that people would go through the agony of the written examination without continuing on to actually *obtain* a valid license? I knew that Sadism was conceived in France by the Marquis de Sade, but I wasn't aware it was still practiced by his contemporaries in administration.

Along with the request letter, I needed to include the summons to the written test, the CERFA 02 form, a copy of my ID card and include another registered self-addressed stamped envelope. The summons was taken from me by the folks who had delivered my written exam. I pointed this out to them in my reply, fearing it would turn into another tail chasing exchange like with the affidavit. "Give us the paper." "You have the paper." "Give us the paper." "You have the paper."

Luckily, they found the summons. But of course they asked me to once again swear an oath that I wasn't signed up with a traffic school. Who were these people doubling up? I tried to imagine a rogue gang of thugs who each paid €2 000 to their school, then decided "Hey, wouldn't it be funny if we ALSO sent our papers in directly?"

"Yeah, man, that would really screw the administration!"

"He-he. We'll show them that even if we pay someone else to do the work for us, we'll STILL do the job ourselves."

"Woo-hoo, that's right! There's only one word for people who do a boring job twice, and pay for the privilege- a REBEL!"

The DDEA wrote back saying they were working

on a date, and meanwhile passed my file on to the DDT, an organization dealing with the 'territory.' I wasn't sure how the two worked together, or if one was a division of the same department. All I knew was that I had new people to write to. New pen pals!

The DDT provided a list of things I'd need before the driving test. First off, I had a provisional right to drive while accompanied. But not just by anyone. I couldn't go to a driving school, because I swore to God three times, that I wasn't signed up with a school. So, they said I had to get someone else who had the equivalent of instructor training. That's right, not just an adult with five plus years of experience. They said I needed an adult 5-year-license-holder, who had passed *specified 7-hour training*. Here was yet another way the *auto-écoles* had put a chokehold barrier to entry to their business. There was no chance I was going to ask any of my friends to sit through that hell. I simply ignored it, and kept on driving solo with my California license. Next requirement.

Secondly, I couldn't use a car of my choice to pass the driving portion. It had to be a special automobile, with '*double commandes*' or dual controls. The passenger side would have a brake and clutch of its own. At any moment, the examiner could stop the car, or neutralize the gears preventing acceleration or deceleration.

Each mirror would also have a twin, facing so the examiner could see what the driver saw. Imagine how disconcerting that would be to operate a vehicle so equipped. It's like driving in the fun house hall of mirrors. Everywhere I looked there were double the cars and double the pedestrians. To avoid stressing out, I'd have to chew some Doublemint gum.

I was instructed that I couldn't drive the dual control car to the test myself. Oh, no no no no. I'd have to bring an adult licensed driver with me. Or, rather a friend would have to drive me as a passenger to the test. This new car, completely unfamiliar to me, would be what I'd be forced to use for the test. I wouldn't get to practice with it either, because my friend didn't have the authorization. Not only would I have to request a personal day off, and get it approved by my company prior to the date, but I'd have to get one of my buddies to do the same. No buddy, no test.

Lastly, the special dual control car would require special insurance. My own auto coverage policy wouldn't do. The policy would have to be faxed to the DDT prior, along with the name and license number of my friend. Without these things, I shouldn't bother showing up.

The DDT said that the examiner could decide to stand me up, if they wanted, without notifying me beforehand. If the examiner felt there was too much snow, or ice, or flooding or fog, they reserved the right to just not show up. This was not the Pony Express.

How would the candidates know how much was 'too much?' They wouldn't. Could you find out before picking up the dual control car and your buddy? Maybe. You could call. No guarantees. You might hear nothing, go down there and see nothing, and if that's upsetting, well, you can say nothing. That's evil.

I got a summons for a test in a nearby town and set the wheels in motion. I was granted a PTO. I lined up the double-commande car rental-Cost: €100 (plus a deposit check of €500) for a half-day. I got special insurance for the car. Finally, my friend Fatima agreed to accompany me. She'd take the day off work as well, to do nothing. Just sit there as a witness. Could you imagine a role less rewarding?

Anyway, with days to spare, I was ready. Or so I thought.

CHAPTER THIRTY-SEVEN

Borne 900 - Schoolmarm test

Examen Monitrice vielle fille

Her thin arms squeezed an impeccably organized file folder to her formless chest. She might have been 25, but dressed like a woman twice her age. Hair yanked back in a bun, collared white shirt buttoned to the earlobes. Tan sweater, plaid skirt all the way down to her flat shoes. Catholic girls start much too late.

A nod. No handshake. She walked stiffly to the car

and avoided eye contact. I could tell she was determined to make up from her youth by showing she knew the code book better than the author. She climbed into the shotgun seat and finally spoke, demonstrating her authority and putting me in my place from the get-go.

"So, you're the student who's here to have me verify your aptitude at driving in order to obtain a permit?" It was as if she was reading from a script.

"I actually do have a license, and I've been driving probably longer than you've been alive." For some reason, this comment seemed to start our relationship off on the wrong foot.

My friend Fatima cringed in the rear-view mirror.

"Anyway. Yes, I am here to have you verify that my drivers license should be validated in France."

She pursed her lips, jotted something in her book and asked me to complete the standard pre-trip verifications which everyone naturally makes before starting off. I played around with the mirrors and adjusted my seat back. I twiddled the belt and had a cursory view with wide exaggerated eyes around the inside of the car. I had no idea what I was supposed to be doing, but tried my best to play up my concern for procedure and safety.

I pulled out into a residential street at the pace of an *escargot*. She asked me to pick up speed. No preamble to our courtship. She wanted me to get right to it. I could roll with that.

The trouble started at the very first intersection.

As we approached a green light the car in front of us inexplicably stopped in the middle of the intersection. I was forced to halt with the nose of my car over the line. The car behind me was on my bumper. The forward car in the intersection then decided to continue at precisely the time the light turned yellow. I was in no-man's land.

I decided immediately to press on the gas and unblock my car from the intersection, likely making it through before the light turned red. She didn't press on her passenger-side brake pedal to stop me, so I saw that as a sign of approval for my decisiveness. She must like a man who takes the bull by the horns.

"Normally, one stops at yellow lights," she said and made a note in her book. I took that for a reprimand but not necessarily outright elimination. The back seat expression said we might as well go home now.

So, thinking I was OK, I asked her what was next. Only then did I notice two of her charming habits which would make my test a delight. She had a very bookish way of speaking, saying three complicated words when one simple word would suffice. And her instructions were delivered so slowly that I had perhaps a second of reaction time.

"We shall forthwith merge onto the motorway."

"Uh, which direction?" We were about a second away from the West on-ramp on the right.

"I should like to ask you to turn left." I flipped my signal and crossed over two lanes through heavy traffic to the left hand turn lane, covering 100 feet. We entered the *Nationale* without incident, and took the first exit.

We pulled out of traffic into a residential square, and the examiner said, "Now you may perform your voluntary maneuver."

"'Voluntary maneuver?'" I snorted, "What's that?"

"I cannot tell you."

"I'm not asking you to do it for me, just to name it

so I know what you're talking about."

"I cannot do that. You should know, *monsieur*."

We began our second lap around the square.

"Can I ask my friend, in the back seat?"

"*Non*. It's covered in the 20 hours of driving time with your driving school."

"Which I didn't have, as you know, *mademoiselle*. I'm an independent candidate. I'm not signed up with a driving school, as I informed your administration a half-dozen times. So could you please..."

"*Non, c'est impossible.*"

I muttered to myself in English that she was a peach, or some other such fruit with a heart as hard as a peach pit. She was playing hard to get. "I know how to handle a dame like that," I thought.

After a breath, trying a sweeter tone. "You know I'm not from around here, I don't know all the terms, and haven't had the benefit of learned instruction from a seasoned professional like yourself. So, if you wouldn't mind schooling me and provide a hint..."

"*Impossible, monsieur.*"

Lap three or four. I noticed a resident in a frilly pink bathrobe frowning at us from behind her red geranium-lined balcony. She must have thought I was a picky parker.

"How about I name a bunch of random stuff I read in the book, and you tell me when I've hit on a winner, OK? *Appel sonore?*"

"*Monsieur*, don't honk! We're in a residence!"

"*Démi-tour?*"

"*Vous voyez bien*, there is not adequate space to make a U-turn here."

"*Créneau?*"

A hesitation. "*Oui, par exemple.*"

Success! I was starting to know what she wanted. I would give it to her.

I've never been so happy about being given the opportunity to parallel park. That's the term in English, of course, 'parallel' which indicates a direction as it relates to a line. The other terms in English are of course diagonal and perpendicular, familiar to anyone who's seen an x/y graph in high school.

Not so in French, where the parking terms are respectively *créneau, épi* and *bataille*. These refer to simple, everyday things you come across- in medieval warfare. A *créneau* is a tall narrow space in the battlements or ramparts of a castle from which you shoot at the enemy. Arrows are the weapon of choice here, which is where *épi* comes from: defined by the arrow head and the way the feathers cross the stick: diagonally. The army you're shooting at is aligned shoulder-to-shoulder, in rows, also known as the position of *bataille*. Nobody uses these terms today to describe how a car is parked. They're only for passing the code, and then forgotten. Except by my military *monitrice*. There would be blood on the battlefield.

I put the Renault in reverse, looked over my right shoulder and started back to parallel park. I placed my right hand on the back of her headrest and heard her shudder. Her breathing quickened as she raised her left hand to her breast. I pretended to pay no attention. Mine was not to wonder why. In a soldierly fashion, I wrapped the Renault's back end around a tight turn, and pulled in-between two parked cars. I stopped with my wheels six inches from the curb.

"You would do well to start from two car lengths in front of the space prior to backing into the vacant spot."

"Have you ever parked in Paris?" I countered. "If you leave that much room, someone will come up behind you and immediately steal your spot." We were each preaching to the unconverted. Lecturing to the unbelieving student. Only one of us would be graded at the end.

The rest of the test went swimmingly. My right rear tire swam over a curb. I lapped the course as I missed turns asked of me tardily, and backstroked to start again. We passed an intense, passion-filled 35 minutes together. I needed a cigarette after.

We returned to our point of departure and got out of the car. The *monitrice* handed me a yellow paper and nodded, all the while keeping her cool grey eyes fixed on mine. Her stone face did an excellent job of concealing the welling up of emotions she must have felt inside. She was used to pimple-faced kids five years her junior tramping uneasily in her domain. Here, at last, was a grown man, with decades of road experience, demonstrating the skill and poise she so often sought in her candidates, in vain. What pretext would she find to renew our fleeting acquaintance?

A week later, a letter informed me that I failed the exam. Not one, but two automatic elimination errors were noted- the light and the curb.

I knew it! Here was proof she had a thing for me. She wanted me to ride her around again.

My friend Fatima passed- on the opportunity to watch me screw up anew. I'd have to find another passenger *pigeon*.

CHAPTER THIRTY-EIGHT

Borne 925 - Gimme a chance, man

Donnez-moi ma chance, merde!

After failing the driving test, students in France have to wait an average of 98 days before they get another chance. That's more than double the European average of 45 days. However, if you're a *libre* candidate, who doesn't go through the *auto-école*, the wait can be up to 24 *months*.

Each of the 10 000 *auto-écoles* have a quota attributed to them, based upon how many successful candidates they've submitted in the past. The smaller the school, or the worse the students' results, the fewer places they get. But since there aren't enough spots to go around in the first place, by the time one is given to a FREE candidate, *mille bornes* have blown by.

Luckily, I didn't need to wait two years before hearing the call. It came the next year, in 2012. The Mayas said the world would end in 2012. If they were right, I sure didn't want to spend the waning moments of the planet meeting the requirements of an administration in a country which would soon cease to exist.

The notice arrived in the Spring. It was for an opportunity to take the driving test in a town 50 kilometers to the East. Candidates don't get to pick the place, nor the date. I wrote back indicating that wasn't convenient for me, and asked for a new date closer to home. A couple months later, a new notice arrived, for a testing spot 50 kilometers to the South. That didn't work either. I didn't hear from them for awhile. Why couldn't they just talk to me on the phone, and we could each look at our agendas and settle on a date?

I returned from vacation on August 6th to find a new notice waiting for me. Miracle of miracles, they offered a test right near my home! It was too good to be true. The test date they scheduled was for August 2nd. Doesn't it figure. I don't hear from them for months, and then a couple days after I leave for vacation, after the *whole country* leaves on vacation, their notice arrives for a date one week hence.

My next notice didn't arrive until December. They proposed a test nearby... during Christmas vacation. I wasn't going to be around, so I wrote to them asking for the same location in January. Eureka! That's just what I got. I shouldn't have been so thrilled.

The morning of my scheduled driving test on Jan 23, 2013 I called just to make sure it was on. A guy came on the line informing me that there would be no tests held that day. They were all canceled because the examiners were on strike.

Returning to their jobs, they must have wanted to prove that, even when protesting, they were really conscientious workers. I got my next test date in a World Record turnaround of two weeks! The morning of February 6, 2013, I awoke to the sight of a thick blanket of snow. The summons stated that tests could be canceled without warning if the weather was bad. I needed to know before dragging another friend and the rental car out there. I called repeatedly into the center and finally managed to reach someone. He confirmed that all the tests were canceled due to snow.

How many more times would this Charlie Brown ask Lucy to setup that football?

Speaking of *masculine - feminine* communication challenges... One evening around this time, my wife went out with colleagues while I stayed home. She took the train to Paris, and didn't come back until late, long after the trains had stopped running. I was a bit concerned, since she hadn't answered my calls, but she arrived home around 1:30 a.m., too tired to speak English. The following Franglish conversation ensued.

"Hey, great, you're home. I was starting to worry. How did you get back? Did someone drive you?"

"*Oui, Uber.*"

"Hubert? What about Nadine?"

"*Nadine n'aime pas conduire la nuit.*"

"Oh, she doesn't like driving at night. Is Hubert from around here?"

"*Non, il est dans mon téléphone.*"

"In your phone? You mean you called him? He wasn't with the group, but then you phoned him to join you? Must be an outsider. Is Hubert new?"

"*Quoi?*" she said distractedly, putting away her coat.

"I mean, he's a colleague I've never heard of before. Is he also in the French department?"

"*De qui tu parles?*"

"Hubert, the guy who drove you back."

"*J'ai pris Uber.*"

"You took him? I thought Hubert drove you. It was Hubert's car, right? Our car was here in the driveway the whole time. Was Hubert too drunk to drive?"

"*Non, c'est toi qui m'a dit d'aller avec Uber.*"

"I said nothing of the sort. Why would I tell you to go home with a man I've never met? I'd never even heard of him before tonight, which makes me wonder…"

"*C'est U-ber. Uuuuuuuu-ber!*"

"I don't care who he is, he's a stranger to me, and I'd just like to know…"

"*Enfin! Eew-bey-ugh-air! UBER!*"

"Are you spelling in English or French, because I don't understand."

"*Tu comprends rien. Je suis fatiguée. Je vais me coucher.*"

"Fine, go to bed. It's not like I'm still looking for an explanation or anything."

Since I wasn't doing too well with the *deuxième sexe*, I

chose a male companion for the next of my 12 labors.

CHAPTER THIRTY-NINE

Borne 950 - Start-sky and Hutch

Start-sky et Hutch

During the Winter school break, my brother-in-law
Philippe paid us a visit. I asked him to stick around an extra
day for my next scheduled driving test date. He accepted,
thinking that he wouldn't be needed. The snow fell all
afternoon, and my appointment was scheduled for the next
morning at 11 a.m. Calling the examiners' office in advance
was no good, because they'd only give information for that

day's activity.

"All tests were canceled for today due to snow. I can't say about tomorrow. You'll have to call back then."

We arose early, just in case. Small flakes persisted in their descent, joining a bed a couple inches deep in the driveway. I planned to call when the office opened at 9 a.m., but it didn't look good.

Meanwhile, I treated my guests to an exotic American breakfast: Lucky Charms and Cap'n Crunch. These are not sold in France, where tartines of toast and jam, or a pot of yogurt are more common than a bowl of cereal. I had brought the packs back from the US, taking them out of the cartons to make better use of precious suitcase space. Looking at my bags ready to leave California, my sister Jenny remarked that it looked like those valises that drug lords opened when exchanging contraband for cash. Sure enough, picking up my luggage in Paris, I discovered a note inside from the TSA, informing me my bag had been opened in transit for inspection. I could just imagine the look on the TSA agent's face. "Yes! I finally got one!" -turning quickly into disappointment upon closer examination. "Green clovers? Blue diamonds?"

Our bellies full of sugar, and the clock striking 9 bells, I tried the office again. No answer.

The conversation turned to Philippe's drive home. It's normally six hours with a stop for food and gas, but might take longer in this weather. My test would retard his departure until at least noon, meaning some night driving on the home stretch. If he could leave now, sundown on the freeway would most likely be avoided.

I didn't want him delayed unnecessarily. Calling the office again at 9:15 produced no response. Nor did the next three dials. I was ready to call the whole thing off, but Philippe kindly encouraged me to try again. At 9:45 somebody finally answered.

"Hi, could you please confirm if the snow has stopped the tests today?"

"No, they're on today. Regular schedule."

Panic!

We ran to the car as the lyrics to the theme song from *Starsky et Hutch* started blaring in the background. What's that? You don't remember the words to the theme song? Oh, that's because the American version didn't have any. But everyone in France can sing the chorus of the French version for you. "*Starrrskeeee et Utch, Nin-nin-nin-nin-nin-nin-nin…*"

Back to the chase…

We took off in the Passat. The *double-commande* car rental place was about 20 minutes away, in the opposite direction of the rendez-vous point for the test. If we grabbed the *double-commande* car within five minutes of arriving, and it took 25 minutes to drive back to the test area, that meant we would be there at 10:35- plenty of time before the test.

The calculations reassured me, and so I took fewer risks on our village streets, which hadn't been swept of snow. The salting had begun on the road leading out of town, so I sped up. Arriving on the main road, we merged into the flow of the regular commute. Traffic was a lot slower, and much later than usual. "All these people are late for work. What the hell are they still doing here? I can't be late for my test!"

I thought about alternate routes. They would take even more time. 10:05 ticked. 10:10. 10:15. The clock sped on, we stayed still and my calculations went out the windshield. Philippe used his mobile phone to call the examiner, and warn them we might be late. No answer.

More cars merged into my lane from the right. The left lane was for turning only. Nothing to do but grin and bear it.

Finally, our turn came up and we whisked away from the bumper-to-bumper commute traffic into the residential district of Rueil-Malmaison. At 10:35, we arrived at the pickup spot. By now, the rental guy recognized me, and I knew the drill, so we were in and out in three minutes.

As I ran off with the keys to a Renault Clio, he reminded me that "the student must be in the passenger's seat until he's with the examiner."

"Don't worry, I have a California license," I said.

"*M'ouais*, but if the examiner sees you driving up, he might dock you points before you even start, or refuse to test you outright."

"It's a chance I'll have to take," I shouted out the rolled-down window. My front wheels spun as I sped off like a bat out of hell. By now, the snow had melted on most of the streets as the temperature rose to five degrees celsius. The road was wet, but not icy. Continual precipitation over previous days had carried away most oils from the road, so it gripped sufficiently. I needed to know quickly what were the limits of this unfamiliar car and its tires on these empty neighborhood roads. There were busier streets up ahead that I'd have to navigate.

As I sped from town to town, every once in a while, I'd catch the horrified expression of a resident. My rental had bright painted letters all around, and a roof banner, clearly identifying it as a trial vehicle for the *auto-école*. There was a big 'A' sticker in the rear window, identifying me as a newby driver. Folks would assume that Philippe, in the passenger seat, was my instructor, condoning my reckless behavior. Everyone is used to seeing these school cars driving slowly, hesitating and holding up traffic. Here I was pushing this tortoise like a rally car. Luckily, I was going too fast for anyone to take down the number.

I downshifted into the main road, egging on the engine to higher speed. The cars opposite were still lined for miles moving at a snail's pace. The main rear-view mirror showed no one following and no police. The second rear-view mirror displayed the wide-eyes of my brother-in-law, scrutinizing for possible danger ahead. I revved into the 5K RPM red-zone before changing gears. I knew there were no radar cameras on this stretch of Nationale.

The straightaway allowed me to make up minutes, but would they be enough? As we pulled off the Nationale into regular city streets, the clock showed 11:00. Still within the window of fashionably late, I thought. Nothing starts exactly on time in Latin countries anyway. Besides, the *last* time my test was scheduled, I had to wait until 11:10 before the examiner returned with the test-taker before me. That time, when we finally left at 11:15, there was another candidate waiting after me. I imagined, at worst, today they'd take the guy scheduled after me first, and I'd wait another half-hour for my turn.

Hope sustained me as the minutes ticked and the parked cars whizzed past my peripheral vision. Nothing but single-lane residential streets remained, all with solid white lines preventing overtaking. I tried the route of fewest streetlights, opting for roundabouts, to continue pressing on, always moving.

At 11:15, I saw the entry to the parking lot of the test area, and slowed to regulation speeds. It was a blind turn and I had my eyes peeled for the examiner, lest they see me behind the wheel. The coast was clear...

Too clear. There wasn't another car in the lot. The previous test must be running over, as usual. We got out and waited maybe a minute before I got too antsy and needed to go somewhere to verify. My pulse was still well over the speed limit.

I asked Philippe to stay lookout while I went to the nearby government building. Here is where they informed me last time that I should just wait in the parking lot. This time, they said that the examiners don't have an office in the building. They just come and go on the lot.

"Well, do you know where the examiner is now?"

"I saw him this morning in the lot, but I don't know now if he's out with a student, or if he left."

"Can you reach him," I implored.

"No, we don't have his number. I don't even know his name." It's true, the examiners have this special hush-hush status, supposedly to avoid any fraternizing or preferential treatment for candidates of colleagues or acquaintances. I was neither, and so saw this evasiveness in the same sense as the condemned sees the hood worn by the executioner.

"You'll have to call the main switchboard."

I went outside and dialed. I held the phone to my ear while looking around to see if they had returned. From across the lot, Philippe shook his head and shrugged. I rejoined him and dialed the dispatcher. About five minutes were necessary to reach a human- who politely explained that all hope was lost.

"There's no one scheduled after you today. The examiner must have gone."

"Well, they can't be very far. Can't you call them back? Especially after all I've gone through to get here. I took time off work, brought a volunteer who meets your criteria and rented a special car at great expense, just for this day."

"*C'est impossible, monsieur.*"

"What? The examiner can be late, but I can't?" I went into a litany about strikes, snow and scheduling in out-of-the-way places. I appealed to his sense of duty as a public servant, as a citizen, as a human being.

"I can't do anything for you, *monsieur.*" He couldn't even re-schedule. I'd have to write another letter to the agency, expressing my intention to continue the process, whereby they'd reply with another arbitrary date and place I'd have no part in choosing.

There was no use in delaying Philippe further, so I dropped him off at home, before driving back alone to return the Clio. It was best that only the interior of the rental heard what I had on my mind.

CHAPTER FORTY

Borne 975 - My Marianne takes charge

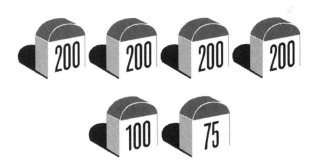

My Marianne takes charge

"This has gone on long enough!"

My wife had her right fist raised. She looked like that Delacroix painting of Marianne, the symbol of the burgeoning French *République*. Well, except for the fact that she had her shirt on. Anyway, her expression was quite dramatic. She was ready to lead a *Révolution*.

"I will go with you to your next driving test. And

this time, you will get it, dammeet!"

With support like that, how could I fail? Really, the driving should have been the easiest part. I've been driving for 30 years, for Chrissakes. Ten in this very country. I just need to do what I know how to do naturally. Go slowly and methodically. Prepare. Schedule at the same place to take the route I've already gone through. Show up on time. Don't talk back.

In preparation, every trip together with my wife to run errands became an opportunity to critique my driving style. In other words, it was like every other trip we've taken with me behind the wheel, only more so.

The wife quizzed me on the signs we saw, the road markings. She made me say out loud what I was thinking about situations with other cars. She forced me to make exaggerated head motions when a quick glance would do. I head-checked every side street on the right like a wigged-out Max Headroom. I had to learn to act the part.

Finally, the notice came in the mail and we both took the morning off. The examiner was a guy this time, middle-aged. His brows went up at first glance of me. "C'mon," he must've thought. "This can't be the guy I'm supposed to test, can he?" Then he smiled and we shook hands.

His voice put me at ease. The test itself was uneventful. It was like taking a Sunday ride with no particular place to go. We went over the exact same route the schoolmarm had me do. My new examiner never commented on the way I handled the car, and gave me plenty of time to react to each instruction. I didn't run into any weird situations with other cars behaving badly, no weather challenges, no road works forcing me into a detour.

It was over before I knew it.

We parted and I turned to Aurore. "Well, that went pretty well, I think."

"Are you kidding? Oh my God, I had to bite my tongue the whole time! It was so hard to keep a calm face in the back seat with all the errors you made."

"Really? I can't think of…"

"You did X and then Y and even Z! *Nobody* does Z!!! I can't believe you did so many mistakes after all the practice we made."

My relief vanished as I started to wonder if my wife's interpretation was more accurate than my own. I really really really didn't want to do the driving test again. This had been going on for a decade, *sacre bleu*!

The days rolled on. Each time I walked away from the mailbox empty-handed.

Finally, a letter arrived with the multi-colored form sent from the examiner. There were X's in yellow and green columns, and O's circling bonuses for courtesy. The most important part was in the upper-left, where 'Insufficient' was crossed out, and 'Favorable' was circled.

It added up to a 21.5 score. It was barely over the passing mark of 20. I didn't care. This American's long international nightmare was over.

"He let you off easy," said my supportive better-half.

CHAPTER FORTY-ONE

Borne 1000 - Back to the starting line

Retour à la case départ

Two months after my last driving test, I finally received my official French driver's license in the mail. It was now December of 2013. A man ten years my younger stared back at me from the photo ID. What was he thinking? His half-smiling expression assured the viewer he was unafraid to take on a challenge. Certainly, he couldn't have imagined a decade-long ordeal.

I was welcomed into the world of officialdom like a fresh-faced newbie. My initial period would start with only six points, instead of the normal 12 points for veteran drivers. I'd have to go three years without any tickets to work my way up to 12-point respectability.

Oh, and during this three-year 'probationary' period, I was asked to display a scarlet letter '**A**' on my rear window. "It's not what you think, wifey." Smiley face ;-) It stands for 'Apprentice,' and warns others that I'm a dopey driver. I ignored this last insult to my dignity, and rolled on without any stinking badges.

Eight months after getting my French license, I was transferred by my company to New York City. Sent by my French employers, I'd be an expat in my own country. I was legal for less than a year in France.

In Manhattan, I wouldn't need a driver's license, much less a French one. Upper-East-Side resident Woody Allen famously never got a driver's license, relying on taxis, public transport and the multitude of other options in a major metropolitan area he rarely left. I wouldn't get a car in New York either. One of my licenses would be dusted off for trips out-of-town.

At least the ten-year troubles served one purpose. Now, when I get pulled over in the 'States, I can show my French license. "Send ze ticket to Uropp, officeur," I will say, in my best fake accent. Just like I'll show my California license in France, with my real 'Rican-ized French shining through. Or, I *would* flash the California license if there were any occasion to do so. The radar Robocops are the only gendarmes you ever 'see' giving a ticket in France. I can now have a perfect driving record everywhere I go.

And this can go on indefinitely, since the French license doesn't expire!

Er, that was, until a *new* system was introduced, only three months before I got my pink French license. I was one of the first lucky laminated to get a digitized card, one which expires after only 15 years. All the privileged souls before me have their immortal pink paper grandfathered without an expiration date.

As for me, check back in 2028 to see if anyone's caught on to my scheme, and if I still have a French License.

Epilog
Epilogue

Future generations will say to me, "No kidding?
You wasted all that time and energy, memorized hundreds
of new terms, spent thousands of dollars, in order to earn
the right to do something you already knew how to do?
How stupid is that? Today, we all get around in self-driving
vehicles. Who needs a driver's license? I might as well start
learning how to knit myself a Roman tunic!"

"Actually, sonny, in the '90s, before smart phones
with keyboards, I had to learn a new way of writing the
alphabet with a stylus so my Palm Pilot could understand
what I wrote."

"How many useless things do you know?"

Young people across the world are reaching the
conclusion that a driver's license is no longer a necessity.
A University of Michigan study from 1983 to 2014 showed
a 47-point percentage drop in 16-year-olds with driver's
licenses in the US. Fewer drivers were also found in their
early 20s and early 30s. The New York Times ran a story in

2013 about the end of car culture. In 'Driverless,' the authors question when adolescents will become adults when there's no longer any rite of passage for getting a driver's license at 16.

Driving school signups in France have similarly dropped 10% in the last five years. Less than 60% of 18-25-year-olds in the Paris region have a driver's license. Why go through the hassle if they can just hitch a ride in a BlaBlaCar?

Of those who DO drive, fewer desire to own. People can rent cars from their neighbor, from the City, from their train provider at their local station. Owners who tried these services, subsequently sold their cars in 46% of cases. In the US, of Americans that sold or changed their cars over the past year, 9% began relying solely on ride services instead of buying a new vehicle.

Of owners in France, more and more are sharing their vehicles to make their car payments. No use having their asset unused 90% of the time, costing them money while rapidly depreciating. Owners pocket 70% of the rental fee, which nets in some cases more than €400 per month. With lock boxes on the drive shaft connected to the app, and photos uploaded before and after, the owner doesn't even need to bother with exchanging keys and verifying damage. More than 25 000 French car owners are convinced to forego ownership, and instead rely on the sharing economy.

These stats are a mirror held up to me, reinforcing the uselessness of my effort to obtain a French driver's license, and asking me if I'm a man behind my times.

Post-script
Post-scriptum

After getting my French license, I drove by the building which housed my old *auto-école*. They had gone out of business. A seedy nightclub had moved in. It would take a helluva lot of drinking and dancing to reverse the karma of that place.

When I finished the whole process, I never wanted to look at another code book again.

I didn't have any sense of accomplishment, no relief. It was like getting a high school diploma, a generation after your classmates. Like receiving a passport so long withheld- to visit your own familiar neighborhood. I no longer felt like a criminal out on parole, closely observed to see if I'd make one false move. I felt like a fool.

I had fallen into the trap. I was a wrinkled, grey-whiskered trained seal, long from the circus, brought back in front of the jury to perform all the old tricks in my repertoire, this time with a ball colored *bleu, blanc, rouge*. Why didn't I exit stage left?

All other 49 US states will trade a California driver's license for their own. 18 of those states have exchange agreements with France. Colorado is the closest of these to California. A round-trip seat can be had for $200. That's at least ten times less than I paid for the process in France. However, they require proof of residency, and I don't know anyone in Colorado.

I *do* have family in New Hampshire, but I didn't ask them to vouch for me. Seemed a petty request from a distant relative. Plus, I thought I'd find another solution.

Maybe another European nation would accept my California Driver's License? I never found such a country. I'd heard Spain and Belgium have simpler processes. My *VBS ruled out Spain. I looked into Belgium. It didn't seem any easier to pass, and a lot more complicated logistically.

The UK was right out. The understandability of the language was far outweighed by the reputed difficulty of the British exam, with the added Hazards Perception test. And of course the steering wheel and the gears are on the wrong side.

So, I waited out the process. Maybe France and California, in a summit meeting of the world's 6th and 7th largest economies, would work out an agreement? They didn't. Maybe I'll move back? I didn't, well, until NYC. The four walls of bureaucracy closed in. The water temperature was raised ever so slowly until this frog was boiled.

I only just learned before publishing that I could have thrown money at the problem. When I told acquaintances that I was writing a book, two people told me they went through the entire preparation process in English (all tests are still in French), both with the Fehrenbach Driving School. One was an Apple employee, and all expats who worked at Apple France were given (at least in the 1990s) free instruction as part of their benefits package. This was worth about 6 000 francs at the time. Today, Fehrenbach's site lists a menu of offerings which by my calculation add up to at least €1 400. At €53 per hour of minimum 8 hours behind-the-wheel time with an instructor, the final figure can become much more. It seems outrageous to a newcomer, but their price isn't really a premium compared to what the standard French-language school costs anyways. I'm sorry to say I ended up paying more by going it alone. Not to mention taking me ten years.

The former employee said that even with English-language preparation, still at least half the Apple folks had to take the tests multiple times before passing. She mentioned brilliant colleagues, like executive directors and lawyers who had graduated from MIT or the University of Michigan just barely getting an acceptable mark, passing by the skin of their noses on the French *examen*.

Unaware of the existence of English-language *auto-écoles* at the time, my will bended to the administration, and I tried to play the cards I was dealt as best I could in a *système complètement franco-français*.

But something else happened in that lost decade.

While I was struggling to meet requirements, I was treated by the administration just like any other person in this country. That is, like a cog in a wheel. I reacted the same way as my fellow citizens, by rebelling, before quietly acquiescing. Many of my *confrères* inquired about my progress and volunteered help, as if it was a common cause. They didn't treat me like an idiot who couldn't hang with their system. We were in it together AGAINST the system. I was welcomed as a part of the band of brothers who wouldn't leave a casualty behind. *Fraternité*.

When I first arrived in France, and saw oncoming drivers *flashing me, warning that the gendarmes had a checkpoint ahead, I was appalled at the gesture. "Maybe they're warning a drunk driver who's a danger to us all. He deserves to be caught," said my puritan self, who believed in truth, justice and the American way- that is, I thought individualistically. Now, I was on the side of my new countrymen. Not an outlaw, but one of US, not one of THEM.

I became a *conducteur citoyen*. In a way, the process to earn my French license had given me license to become French.

Stats
Statistiques

Time it took to obtain my French license
10 years, 3 months (September 2004-December of 2013)

Time off work
PTO days expended: six

Cost of getting my French license
Driving school, books, study materials: €800
Special 'double-commande' Car rentals to take test: €400
(€100 x 4)
LRAR: €100 (at least 20 registered letters at €5 a pop)
Fuel to/from school and prefecture: €200
Translation of US documents: €77
Photos: €30 (at least 3x at €10 a pop)
Total: €1607

Get your filthy 4-wheeler out of my pristine Paris
Sortez-moi cette espèce de poubelle à 4 roues de mon Paris impeccable!

Change happens slowly, but if you stick around long enough, you can see it take place, even in France.

Progress is happening in the liberalization of the driving school system. New online players like Ornikar and Lepermislibre have popped up, lowering costs. The government has allowed many more examiners to take part, from places like the post office, shortening wait times. La Poste made €20M from automobile tests in 2017. The site VroomVroom helps you compare schools.

Subsidies have risen greatly for purchasing an electric car. You can more easily get rid of your old jalopy by using PayCar and Depopass to sell your car.

If you don't want to own because the €5 796 average annual cost is too high, many car-sharing services such as Zipcar, Travelcar, Koolicar, Communauto, Ubeeqo, Carlili, Car2go, Citiz, Virtuo and Drivy have appeared on the scene. The Free2Move app lists a round-up of services, and links to book them. Even manufacturers Citroën, Nissan (Renault) and BMW have introduced 'time-share' car leases. The Bluecar from Autolib[1] is a popular self-drive option, to grab-and-go for €0.32 per minute, paid for conveniently by the Parisian transport card, Navigo. Through OuiCar you can rent an SNCF vehicle right at the train station for €15 per day.

Stan is the name of a new a free service at Charles De Gaulle airport to have a robot park your car. It's the least they could do, after all, a day's parking at CDG costs $44. Outside the airport, it's now easier to find a free spot with the App Zenpark. Even private spaces, like somebody's garage, can be purchased through online systems, increasing the woefully inadequate number of spots in Paris.

Convenient and cheaper services now exist to get your car checked. For the bi-annual *contrôle technique*, Avatacar will come to your residence and perform the check. Clikclikcar will pickup your car for you, drive to the check center, and return your car once it's passed. Both services are 20% less expensive than the traditional garages.

Commuters have more options. Even though only 8% of French drivers are willing to carpool, French startup Blablacar has become the leader in the area with BlaBlalignes. Wayzup, Less, IDvroom, Indigo, Citygoo,

OuiHop and Zify also offer home-to-work ride sharing.

Uber, G7 and the Taxis Bleu are hardly the only cab solutions. They've been joined by Marcel, Taxify, Snapcar, LeCab and Chauffer-Privé.

If your thing is more *les deux roues* Cityscoot has you covered. A thousand of their white electric scooters are available all over Paris for €0.28 per minute. Another 600 black scooters are offered by Coup, a unit of Bosch, for even less. In 2018, together they'll grow to more than 3 000 units. As mentioned in the Double Standard chapter, you don't need a license to drive a scooter, but these apps ask you for one at registration.

Employers and the region can also reimburse €0.25 per kilometer for biking to work. More than 300 000 people are annual subscribers to the 22 000 Vélib' grab-and-go bicycles you see everywhere in Paris. This will soon be expanded to the suburbs, with an additional 20 000 bikes. What's more, they'll be all electric, which helps as the communities of the 'couronne' are quite hilly. Many other bike entrepreneurs like GoBee Bike, oBike, Ofo and IndigoWeel have invaded the sidewalks with free-floating fleets.

The outdated paper *Métro* tickets will next year be completely replaced by Navigo, offering the possibility of pay-as-you-go. This option will be coupled with contactless cards and mobile phone payment systems to speed you through the turnstiles just like the Oyster card in London, at less than a quarter of the price. A fleet of 36 all-electric city busses will transport riders in the Yvelines starting in September. Futuristic taxi boats, called SeaBubbles will start moving people on the Seine, propelled by foils lifting them above the water.

Sadly, in most other realms the French roads are becoming more pecuniary and *pénible*. The worst changes are happening to drivers in Paris. Car-sharing service Heetch was shut down by a court decision, forcing them to pay €500K in fines and court fees. The judge saw a big difference between BlaBlaCar's model, where the driver decides the route, and Heech's, where the passenger decides, like in a taxi.

In 2014, Paris elected a new mayor, Anne Hidalgo. She's from the socialist party, or the PS, on the left, so you'd expect her to be more concerned with ecological issues, and have a people-pleasing manner. Well, one out of two. If Ralph Nader had a child with Napoleon, it would be her.

While many residents agree that changes in

transportation should be made toward alternatives causing less pollution and noise, citizens expect advanced notice, to have their views heard, and a time to adapt. That's not what you get with Ms. Hidalgo. She dictates new measures which are confusing to follow, much less adhere to, and they take immediate effect with severe penalties for non-compliance. Her public enemy number one: the automobile.

Auto access to the capital has been drastically reduced. No cars older than 20 years may enter the city limits. That's 10% of all cars. Bus access to the capital has also diminished, as 26% of busses are 20 years old. Mass confusion ensued. It's not as if you can easily sell or exchange your car right away, or easily alter your mode of transportation with a snap of the fingers. Tour groups from foreign countries which plan group excursions months in advance only discovered the new legislation upon entering the city. What a way to welcome tourists to the most visited city in the world. A city which will host the 2024 Olympic Games. Since Ms. Hidalgo's measures began, a new record was set with 484 kilometers of traffic jams around Paris. Commuters spent 90 hours in Parisian traffic jams in 2016, which is 12 1/2 hours more in one year, a 16% increase.

When newer cars and buses finally get into the

city, they're obliged to move at gridlock speeds, whether or not there's any traffic. The mayor wants to lower the speed limit from 50 km/h (29mph) to 30 km/h (18mph) in nearly the whole city. Entire arrondissements I, II, III, IV, V, VI, X, XI, XII, XIII, XIV, XVIII, XIX, and XX would be affected. Some of Paris' only wide thoroughfares run through these neighborhoods, which will turn into slow-moving parking lots, even after 1 a.m., when the trains no longer run, and the city streets are your only way home.

There's fewer places cars can legally go. The widest street in the capital, the Champs-Elysées, becomes pedestrian only on the first Sunday of every month. This isn't widely known, nor is it noted with signs on the way there. You just drive along until you meet a barrier, without any suggested deviation. Then you follow a line of similarly blocked cars into another barrier. There's nowhere for you to go, and no instructions out of the labyrinth. You've just been Hidalgoed!

Every day of *every* month, the three kilometers of lanes along the river, known as *voies sur berge de la Seine*, have been converted to pedestrian-only. While that now makes it a bit nicer to stroll along the banks of the river, it's still visually concrete, asphalt and block walls. Inland from the river, along sidewalk cafés and street benches, is now a maelstrom of motor noise (+125%), honking and exhaust. These major arteries were shut off without thought as to where all the cars would go, 43 000 per day. The result is that in six months, there's been an enormous shift of traffic going by the streets of the interior, taking up to 73% longer to cross. This shift included an overnight 88% increase in traffic on the street passing right in front of City Hall. Maybe the mayor appreciates a close-up view of the mayhem she causes?

How effective are Ms. Hidalgo's measures? Well, for one, reducing the speed limit on all 35 kilometers of the Péripherique from 80km/h to 70km/h has only made things worse. Traffic became bunched up and less fluid, more fuel is consumed, pollution has increased and there are more accidents. There are more tickets issued, so the government's revenues go up, but drivers are unnecessarily penalized and residents receive zero benefit.

A similar measure in the city of Rennes, France was finally scrapped when a study proved no benefit to reducing the speed limit to 70km/h. No bother, Ms. Hidalgo persists, insisting there have been unproven improvements.

Ms. Hidalgo's fellow PS partisan, former environment minister Ségolene Royale, introduced new emissions tagging legislation with the same confusion and lack of preparation. Initially, Paris reacted to pollution peaks by a system called *circulation alternée*, restricting or penalizing cars. Odd license plates were allowed into the city on odd-numbered days of the month. Even on even. But what constitutes odd and even on a French license plate? If it's the last number on a plate, well, entire '*départements*' could be restricted. This is because a large number of license plates in France end with the two numbers which commence their postal code. Folks from the Val-d'Oise (95) must keep their cars out of Paris on even days; folks from the Yvelines (78) must stay out on odd days. And what about those who live in Paris (75)? Must they drive out of the city to park on even days? Isn't the whole idea to get LESS people using cars?

What replaced 'alternate circulation' was a series of five color-coded stickers, called Crit'Air. You go online and type in your car's details, and pay €4.18, then you receive the sticker corresponding to your vehicle's propensity to pollute. You must display the sticker on your car or risk getting fined when you enter Paris. While having very little impact on the quality of the air, Crit'Air does substantially grow the State's coffers. Only five days after its introduction, €4 Million in new funds were collected from drivers. If the government really cared about air pollution, they'd go after air carriers and cruise lines instead. A cruise ship in port pollutes as much as 1M cars.

If you think to yourself, "Crit'Air doesn't affect me because I don't live in the Paris region," think again. It applies to *any* car which drives into Paris, or other major French cities, even once. If you're from Dijon and you drive to Grenoble once a year, they expect you to have the sticker. If you're from the UK, or Belgium or the Netherlands, it applies to your trip to Lyon, too. German cities thought this was such a good idea, they adopted a similar system for Berlin... with a different sticker, of course. Soon European delivery drivers won't be able to see out of their windshield with all the stickers they'll need for every municipality.

An anti-car bombshell was announced in July by Madame Royale's replacement, Nicolas Hulot. By 2040, France plans to outright ban diesel cars, AND all gasoline-powered cars as well. The sale of fuel for these cars will also be prohibited. They expect that in 23 years, 99% of all cars currently on the roads will be replaced by electric, or clean-fuel alternatives. They have too much faith in technology. The internet is around 23 years old. Yet many,

many organizations today are still dependent on legacy systems, notably government agencies.

Security cameras installed on streetlamps can now be used to dole out tickets, without warning. These ones have actual humans behind the screens looking for one false move. In Paris alone, 1 200 cameras have enabled watchful authorities to dole out more than 150 000 tickets for such infractions as not wearing a seatbelt or using a mobile phone behind the wheel. It's not just suspect streets like *la rue de la Grande-Truanderie* (Great Gangsterism road) or *la rue des Mauvais-Garçons* (Bad Boy road). The Parisian police suspect we're ALL criminals. More cameras will be installed near the Charles De Gaulle airport. Big Brother is now *Grand Frère Jacques*, and he's never sleeping.

European states have started sharing data with each other in an attempt to catch radar speeders with out-of-country plates. Employers are now obligated to denounce their employees for radar pictures of a company car speeding.

Private companies are being deployed to manage and increase the number of mobile radars, and use them aboard common cars to trap unsuspecting motorists. In a

2016 test, these unmarked cars flashed 1,9 million times. Now, all 383 cars will be deployed in September 2017, and should easily capture an additional 15 million infractions annually, on top of the 20 million already from the fixed radars. France was already the most pecuniary country in the world for motorists. Now, they stand poised to double the amount they collect from fines in a single year.

A backlash is inevitable. It's starting with an initiative by 40 millions d'automobilistes. The association encourages all concerned citizens to telephone Anne Hidalgo at +33 1 42 76 48 11 and let her know how you feel.

The automobile used to be a symbol of freedom, of pleasure and shared sensations. Today, it's simply the quickest way between point A (the authorities) and point B (your wallet).

Acknowledgements
Remerciements

Doing research for this book made me pore over all the rules and regulations again, all of my study notes, all of my failed practice tests. I had forgotten how humiliating an experience that was. The old feelings resurfaced immediately, and I knew I had re-captured the mood which dominated my disposition at the time. However, that's not the tone I wanted for my book.

None of the situations I experienced made me laugh at the time. But looking back, I could see they were comical. Either the scene was burlesque, or my bumbling was laughable. Whenever I'd relay an anecdote to a friend, they'd stifle a guffaw, then commiserate, because they knew sympathy is what I needed. My ordeal was still going on at the time, and nobody knew if I'd make it through.

Now, I'm OK and I can look back and laugh. This book is an invitation to all who shared my journey to openly laugh with me (instead of privately laughing *at* me): Philippe Davin, Fatima Imbert, Christine Comélèra, Philippe Comélèra, JP and Sylvie Langlet, Sharon Schanzer, Joanna Penn, the fine pensmiths and critics of the Paris Creative Writers meetup especially Gray, Lucas,

Nancy, Conny, Michel, and of course my wife, without whom I'd still be trying to get my French license.

References
Références

In researching while writing this book, I came across travel books of practically all means of transportation: train, low-cost-carriers, sailing, rowing, canal boating, motorbiking, bicycling, on foot, hitch-hiking and of course the automobile road-trip. I didn't find any covering the hassles and foibles of obtaining a driver's license, much less a foreign one.

Maybe that's because it's not a terribly interesting topic. Would I want to read such a recollection? Probably not, if it was described like that.

However, told as a funny story, or an interior journey, I thought it could work. There are many ways to relate comedy, and many everyday situations which cause laughter. To fully appreciate the joke, you have to have been there. So, in bringing you into the scene, going into detail, I hope I've created the build-up to the punch-line.

An interior journey comes about when you stay in one place for a while. It's the opposite of a road trip, which forever pushes onward, constantly changes and leaves yesterday's cares in the dust. A road trip skims along the surface. An interior journey grows roots.

There are many such tales, told from the perspective of the outsider who stays. Tales by the observer who notices what the passer-by misses. He sees the seasons pass, encounters the same people at different times, becomes embedded in his surroundings.

Here is a list of items I've pointed to, and some fellow travelers who've led me to create this piece:

Books
Country Driving by Peter Hessler
Driverless: Intelligent Cars and the Road Ahead, The MIT Press, Hod Lipson and Melba Kurman
Dictionary of French Tools & Materials, Richard Wiles
Jesus Shaves, a short story in the book Me Talk Pretty One Day from David Sedaris
The Knowledge
L'autorefoulement et ses limites by Mathieu Flonneau
Les Bonnes Excuses des Mauvais Conducteurs by Alexandre Despretz
A Short History of Tractors in Ukrainian by Marina Lewycka

Magazines and Newspapers
01net
Alternatives Economiques
Auto Journal
Auto Moto
Auto Plus
Capital
Entreprises et Carrières
Forbes
French Property
L'Express
Le Figaro

Le Parisien and Le Parisien magazine, notably the February 3, 2017 issue

Libération

Mieux Vivre Votre Argent

MIT Technology Review, November-December 2016

Smithsonian magazine

Society magazine, notably the September 16, 2016 issue

The New York Times

The Telegraph

The Wall Street Journal

Time

Washington Post

UFC-Que Choisir

Websites

40 millions d'automobilistes

AccidentSketch diagrams

AdrianLeeds.com

Americans in France

Antai

Autoscout24

Bison Futé

Byebyecrottoir.eu

California Department of Motor Vehicles. "*2016 California Driver Handbook.*" v1.6

Caradisiac.com

Carbuyer UK

chronique de monitrice

CNRS

Droit Finances

Easy Rad

Forum Auto

France-pub.com

Garé comme une merde

linternaute.com

J'aime ma route

Map showing speed limits of road ways in France
MediaSalesExec
Motoservices.com

© OpenStreetMap contributors

Quelpermis.com

Quartz

Quora

Radar blog

Roaditude

Sauvermonpermis.com

Slate.com

Sofres

Video permis

Wikipedia

Wikitravel driving in France

World Health Organization

Biography
Biographie

A little about the author- after graduating with a journalism degree, Joe Start jumped over to the advertising and marketing side of communications. His day job has been selling media and technology in the US and Europe for more than a dozen years, lately with startups. This is his return to writing, with his first book.

His second book, The Chairfather, was released in 2018. The book is an irreverent series of brief encounters over lunch with 50 departed divas decomposing at the cemetery of Père Lachaise. Candid photos. Spicy interviews. Luminaries who haven't spoken for hundreds of years. You'll never believe what they say!

To keep track of Joe Start's creations, please drive over to StartGoingPlaces.com to add your name to his newsletter. You'll learn about what's next, his upcoming appearances and check out bonus material from this book. Please let him know what you thought, and help guide others in their deliberations by reviewing on the usual marketplaces, Goodreads, Colibris, Book Riot, or your own blog.

Subscribe to Start Going Places blog: http://eepurl.com/cVVtJf and get one of his works for free!

Favorite the author at Smashwords: https://www.smashwords.com/profile/view/JoeStartAuthor

Walk with 'The Chairfather' on his VoiceMap tours: https://voicemap.me/authors/joe-start

Follow Joe on Facebook: https://www.facebook.com/JoeStartAuthor